EMILY CAVINS, LISA BROMSCHWIG, REGINA NEVILLE, and LINDA WANDREI

Foreword by JEFF CAVINS

Illustrations by EILEEN MCCOOK

West Chester, Pennsylvania

Storybook

God's Plan in Scripture (GPS) Storybook is a resource of *The Great Adventure* Bible Study Program and Gen2Rev Catholic Bible Studies, LLC.

Published by Ascension Publishing, LLC.

Ascension
PO Box 1990
West Chester, PA 19380
1-800-376-0520
ascensionpress.com

Cover and interior design: Rosemary Strohm
Illustrated by: Eileen McCook

Printed in the United States of America

ISBN 978-1-950784-49-3

To our husbands, Jeff, Kurt, Tom, and Phil, for their support and promotion.

To our children, who participated in our programs.

And to the memory of Fr. Mark Dosh, for his reflective and clarifying edits.

Holy God,

"Open my eyes, that I may behold wondrous things out of your law."—Psalm 119:18

May the Holy Spirit help me to understand your plan of salvation,
through Christ our Lord. Amen.

CONTENTS

Appendix

Foreword

Children love stories. They never seem to grow tired of hearing them, even the same story told over and over again. Throughout their lives, they may hear individual stories from the Bible, but few will grow up understanding how these stories "fit in" with the whole. Without a complete understanding of God's plan for us as told in the Bible, they may end up with a disjointed and incomplete view of God and the Catholic Faith.

Growing up with a true understanding of who God is, who we are, and how we are called to live can be difficult in our current secular culture. Our children will no doubt encounter ideas that are very different from the story given to us in God's Word. This can confuse them and make them uncertain in the Faith. Part of our responsibility as parents and educators is to accurately convey God's Word to the next generation, teaching them to discern truth from falsehood.

In the sixth chapter of Deuteronomy, Moses tells the Israelites, *"These words which I command you this day shall be upon your heart; and you shall teach them diligently to your children, and shall talk of them when you sit in your house, and when you walk by the way, and when you lie down, and when you rise"* (Deuteronomy 6:6-7). If the people of Israel were to be faithful to God in a foreign land, they needed to teach their children his ways. So, too, must Catholic parents diligently teach the Faith to their children so they can remain faithful to God's ways in the midst of a secular world.

Jesus said, *"My sheep hear my voice, and I know them, and they follow me"* (John 10:27). Children come to know the voice of God by hearing it proclaimed in the Bible. The Word of God is like a seed that is planted in young hearts. As it grows, it will accomplish what God wills—a deeper relationship with him.

When children read the Bible with their parents, they are experiencing God's Word with those they trust the most. The Bible gives children wisdom for living, direction for their lives, and comfort in so many ways.

The foundation for everything we believe as Catholics springs from salvation history, the "big story" found in the Bible. If God's children do not know this amazing story, they will not understand their place within it. If a biblical foundation is not built in the hearts of our children, the sacramental life of the Church—especially the Liturgy—will not be seen in light of the whole story. What meaning is there in the Creed or the sacraments if their role in salvation history is not understood?

From reading the Bible, children will come to know the heart of their heavenly Father as well as his amazing deeds for us. In the Bible, they will find examples of how God has worked with people in the past. As they grow older, they will come to see that, since God is eternal and does not change, he can work with them in a similar way.

When we face difficult situations, we need to know that we can turn to God and trust in him. As the stories of the Bible become part of our children's lives, they will receive wisdom and counsel from God's Word and be able to articulate their faith to friends and family.

The Storybook presents the story of salvation in a way that engages kids' minds and hearts. As you read the Bible and the Storybook with your children, they will come to understand the Bible as a story—and learn how this story is fulfilled in Christ and his Church.

What better way to engage our children with Jesus than to read to them the best story ever told? Jesus wants each of his children to hear about his love: *"Let the children come to me, and do not hinder them; for to such belongs the kingdom of heaven"* (Matthew 19:14). We bring our children into the kingdom of God, the Church, through baptism and promise to raise them in the Faith. Taking time to read the Bible is an important way we can fulfill this promise.

In the course of reading the Bible together, parents and their children will not only learn salvation history, but they will also build a memorable relationship with one another rooted in a shared faith. This deepened knowledge of the Catholic Faith can be the subject of discussions at the dinner table, at family gatherings, and on trips.

If our desire is for our children to grow up and change the world—and if we want our children to teach their children—then we must begin now by reading the Bible with our sons and daughters and bringing them into the story. This simple exercise will prove to be some of the best time we have ever spent. So seek to plant God's Word into the hearts of your children and pray that God will do amazing things in their lives.

Jeff Cavins
Creator and President
The Great Adventure Catholic Bible Study Program

Introduction

This book can be used independently or as part of the *God's Plan in Scripture (GPS)* program for an adult and child learning experience. The experience includes reading from a preselected text from the Bible and then reading a summary of that text in the Storybook. As you read this book along with the Bible, it will show you and your child, story by story, the unfolding of the Father's love for us. This book can aid in understanding Scripture as a timeless collection of stories, teachings, and events inspired by God and written for our benefit. This book helps parents to be the primary teachers of their children by walking with them through Scripture, learning the Catholic Faith, and answering the question, "Why should I read the Bible?"

The stories follow the lives of real people—people like us, who were created to know God and love him but who often, instead, turn away from him and go their own way. This act of disobedience, much like Adam and Eve's first sin, separates us from God. The Bible stories show us how God pursues us—and has always pursued us! —despite our sin, teaching us his ways, inviting us over and over again to turn back to him.

Our Catholic Faith in the Bible

This book is unlike any other in that within the context of the narrative, the reader will discover where the basics of the Catholic faith are found in Scripture. This book functions like a "linear catechism" in that the aspects of the Catholic Faith appear chronologically.

Not only is the story of salvation summarized but also the biblical roots of the necessary elements of the Faith are identified, which are found in the Creed, the sacraments, the Rosary, and the teachings of the Church. These connections make the vital links between the Bible, the Mass, and our Faith.

Bible Reading Checklist

This book lays out a Bible reading checklist that follows the chronological flow of the salvation story in the same way as the adult program, *The Bible Timeline: The Story of Salvation*. Each reading selection is one to two chapters of the actual Bible. This book then summarizes that Scripture reading to help readers understand the text. As you progress together through the Bible, you can mark off the portions you have read. If the children are old enough to read the Bible text themselves, encourage them to look up the reference unassisted. This will cultivate the art of finding chapter, book, and verse in the actual Bible.

Catholic Bible

The Storybook aligns with the Catholic Bible. The Scripture quotations are taken from *The Great Adventure Catholic Bible*, which uses the Revised Standard Version, Second Catholic Edition (RSV-2CE), published by Ascension. If you use another version, like the New American Bible (NAB) or Douay-Rheims Bible, you will notice some differences in wording.

WHY ARE CATHOLIC AND PROTESTANT BIBLES DIFFERENT?

In the early days, the Church used a Greek translation of the Old Testament called the Septuagint. This included the thirty-nine books of the modern Jewish canon plus seven books Jews consider sacred but did not later retain in their canon (the "deuterocanonical" books). Catholic Bibles follow the Septuagint and include all forty-six books in their Old Testament, while the Protestant reformers chose to follow the shorter Hebrew canon. The Catholic canon also includes additional text in the books of Esther and Daniel.

CATECHISM OF THE CATHOLIC CHURCH

The *Catechism of the Catholic Church* is a summary of the Church's teachings. It is commonly referred to as the *Catechism* and is usually abbreviated "CCC." It is referenced in parentheses throughout this book. The *Catechism* helps us understand the Bible in the context of the

Tradition of the Church. Reading excerpts from the *Catechism* along with the Bible adds much to the understanding of Catholic teaching and is greatly encouraged.

Text Formatting Key

Bible Quotes	If a Bible verse is quoted, it is marked in italics.
(Citations)	Citations for Bible verses not included on the checklist appear in parentheses in the text.
(CCC)	Citations for references from the *Catechism of the Catholic Church* (CCC) appear in parentheses in the text.
Mass Phrases	Bold italics show Bible verses spoken by the priest or people during Mass.
Glossary	Bolding shows terms defined in the glossary.
Covenant Circles	Indicate God's covenants with his people.
Banners	Show portions of the Nicene Creed.
Crosses	Show the biblical origins of the seven sacraments.
Rosary beads	Show the biblical origins of the mysteries of the Rosary.
The appendix	Contains deeper explanations of these features in more detail.

At the end of each chapter, answer the conversation-starter questions together. They will help you make personal connections with the stories you have read. By reading the Bible and talking about it together, you and your children will develop a deeper relationship with God while also learning about the Catholic Faith.

Nothing is more powerful than a child learning how to navigate and read the Bible with a parent or other caring adult. This witness alone will make a powerful impact on your children's memory, giving them a visible witness of the love of God. As parents and caring adults, you are vital to creating a domestic church through which you teach your children the love of God as revealed in the Bible. The love of our heavenly Father is shared and passed down for generations to come.

"ALL SCRIPTURE IS INSPIRED BY GOD AND PROFITABLE FOR TEACHING, FOR REPROOF, FOR CORRECTION, AND FOR TRAINING IN RIGHTEOUSNESS."

—2 Timothy 3:16

Chapter One

Finding the Story in Scripture

What is the Bible?

The Bible is also called the Word of God or Sacred Scripture. The words in the Bible are **inspired** by God and tell of his loving plan for all people. The words written are therefore true. The Bible is one of the most popular books sold all over the world. Actually, it is more than just a single book: It is a "library" of seventy-three books. God inspired human authors to write the books of the Bible (CCC 105–107). When we hear the Bible readings proclaimed at Mass or when we read the Bible ourselves, we hear God himself speaking to us.

Why do we study the Bible?

We study the Bible so we can know the plan of God for our lives and can experience his great love for each of us. In the pages of the Bible, we learn the story of our salvation, how God planned from the beginning of the world to send a Savior, Jesus, who would defeat sin and death and who would offer all people eternal life with God. The Bible is the guidebook for living as a Christian, so it is important to read and study it.

Who helps us understand the Bible?

We know that God used human beings to write his message. The Holy Spirit continues to help us today to understand what these writers from thousands of years ago have written. When we pray before reading the Bible, the Holy Spirit will guide us. The Church has given us the *Catechism of the Catholic Church* (CCC) as a reference for understanding the Bible in the context of the Church's history and Tradition. We trust that the authors of the Catechism were guided by the same Holy Spirit who guides us today. Guidelines for interpreting Scripture can be found in the *Catechism* in paragraphs 101–119.

How are the books of the Bible arranged?

The books in the Bible are divided into two sections, the Old Testament and the New Testament. A *testament* is a **covenant** or agreement. The Old Testament has forty-six books, and the New Testament, which tells about Jesus Christ and the Church, has twenty-seven books. The first four books of the New Testament are called *Gospels*, which means "good news." The Gospels are especially important because they tell us about the life of Jesus, and we give them special reverence by standing at Mass during the Gospel reading.

Many people try to read the Bible from beginning to end in an attempt to get a complete picture of the overall story, but the Bible's books are not arranged in chronological order. Rather, they are grouped into literary categories such as history, poetry, prophecy, and letters, making it difficult to find the narrative. The Storybook makes it easier to learn God's story by following fourteen narrative books, which present the events of **salvation history** in order.

What is salvation history?

Within the many stories found in the seventy-three books of the Bible, there is one amazing overall story of God's love for us. It is this overall story that we call Salvation History.

The Bible tells how God created everything, including people, and that everything he created was good. *The Catechism of the Catholic Church* explains further: God's plan of sheer goodness gives us a share in his own blessed life (see CCC 1). Sometimes, though, people reject God by choosing to disobey him. This disobedience is called sin. Sin results in separation from God and, ultimately, death.

God in his infinite love makes a way for people to come back to him through his Son, Jesus Christ. Jesus' death on the Cross and his glorious resurrection restored our broken relationship. In other words, God became man in order to free humanity from sin. Jesus ascended into heaven after his resurrection. Then he sent the Holy Spirit to guide the Church as it continues his saving work. This is where we enter the story!

When we are baptized, we become part of the Church, so the story of the Bible is really a story that includes us! It is the best adventure story that anyone could ever imagine, and we are part of it. When we read the Bible, we learn that God loves us and that he wants us to share in his perfect love forever. As you read the Storybook along with the Bible, remember that the biblical heroes like Abraham, David, and the Blessed Virgin Mary are part of your story, too. You are part of their family.

How does *The Great Adventure Bible Timeline* help me read the Bible?

NARRATIVE BOOKS

This Storybook follows *The Bible Timeline*, which organizes biblical history from Creation through the establishment of the Church into fourteen narrative books. These books follow the main events of the story, identifying key people and biblical events.

TIME PERIODS

The fourteen narrative books are arranged into twelve time periods that group the events of salvation history into "chapters."

SUPPLEMENTAL BOOKS

The remaining fifty-nine books of the Bible are referred to as "supplemental books." They support the narrative story with different points of view and additional events. *The Bible Timeline* shows how these books fit into the time periods.

The Bible Timeline

SYMBOL	TIME PERIOD	NARRATIVE BOOKS	SUPPLEMENTAL BOOKS
	Early World	Genesis 1-11	
	Patriarchs	Genesis 12-50	Job
	Egypt and Exodus	Exodus	Leviticus
	Desert Wanderings	Numbers	
	Conquest and Judges	Joshua, Judges, 1 Samuel 1-8	Ruth
	Royal Kingdom	1 Samuel 9-31, 2 Samuel, 1 Kings 1-11	1 Chronicles, 2 Chronicles, Psalms, Proverbs, Ecclesiastes, Song of Solomon
	Divided Kingdom	1 Kings 12-22, 2 Kings 1-16	2 Chronicles, Amos, Jonah, Hosea, Isaiah, Micah
	Exile	2 Kings 17-25	2 Chronicles, Tobit, Judith, Isaiah, Jeremiah, Lamentations, Baruch, Ezekiel, Daniel, Hosea, Joel, Obadiah, Micah, Nahum, Habakkuk, Zephaniah
	Return	Ezra, Nehemiah	Daniel, Zechariah, Haggai, Esther, Malachi
	Maccabean Revolt	1 Maccabees	2 Maccabees, Wisdom of Solomon, Sirach
	Messianic Fulfillment	Luke	Matthew, Mark, John
	Church	Acts	Paul's Letters, Other Letters, Revelation

How do I use the Bible Reading Checklist?

The Bible Reading Checklist directs you to the portions of the Bible to be read for each chapter. Look at the sample below. After the checkbox, a Bible reference gives the name of the book. The verse or verses are listed after the colon (:).

Example:

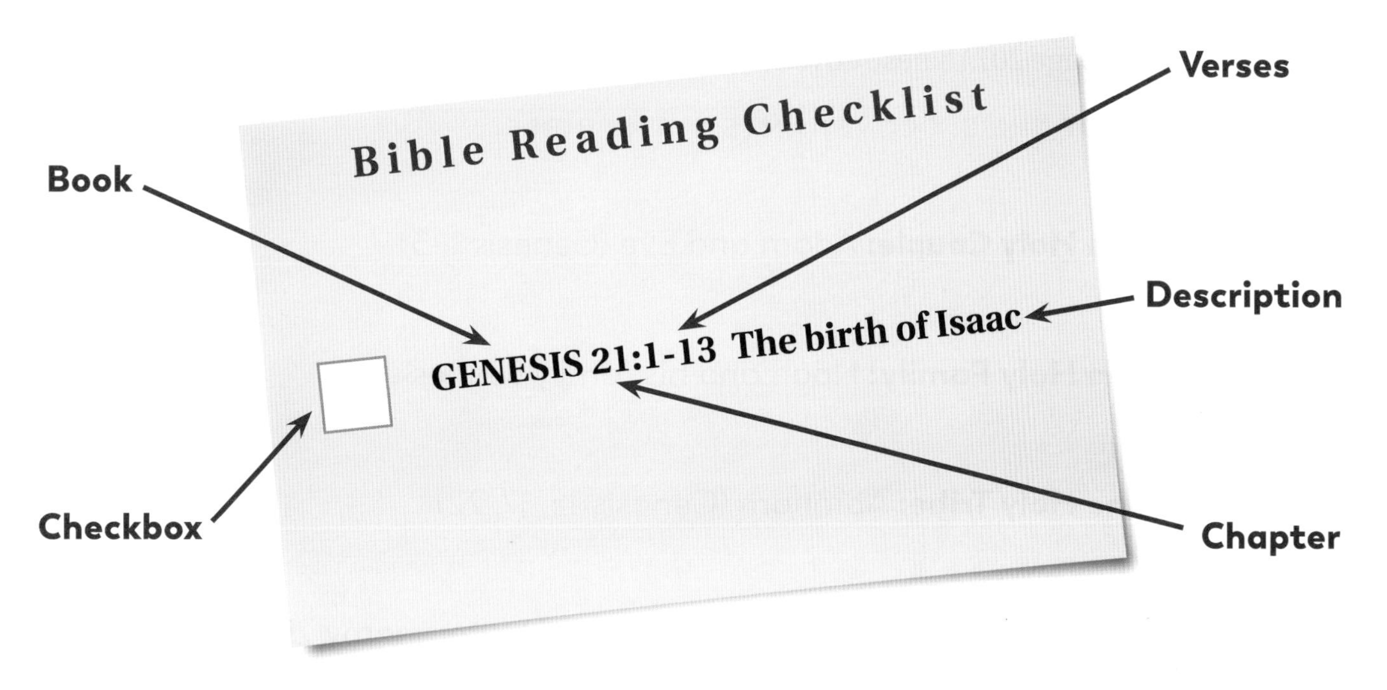

For the example above in chapter 21 of Genesis, read only verses 1-13.

After reading from a particular Bible text, make an "X" in the checkbox and then read the summary portion in the Storybook that has the same scripture reference as the reading description.

Some reading selections are marked as optional. These are familiar Bible stories that provide additional points of view but are not necessary for the flow of the story.

Six Covenants

Another way to follow God's plan for all humanity is to look at the six covenants God made with his people as found within the narrative books of the Bible. A *covenant* in the Bible is an agreement between God and one or more persons. Everyone involved in the covenant promises to do their part by agreeing to the terms of the covenant and by swearing an oath. (The six covenants are defined further in "The Six Covenants Established in the Bible" in the appendix on page 207.) These covenants will appear within a circle in the book.

PROGRESSION OF THE SIX COVENANTS IN THE BIBLE:

One Holy Couple: Adam and Eve (Genesis 1–3)

One Holy Family: Noah and his family (Genesis 9)

One Holy Tribe: Abraham (Genesis 15, 17, 22)

One Holy Nation: Moses (Exodus 24, Deuteronomy 29)

One Holy Kingdom: David (2 Samuel 7:11-15)

One Holy Church: Jesus Christ (Matthew 16:18; Luke 22:1-23)

Beginning the Journey of *The Bible Timeline*

In love, God created the world. We were all created out of that same love in order to be united with God in heaven for eternity. When people sin, it disrupts their relationship with God and with one another. God's answer is found in John 3:16: *"For God so loved the world that he gave his only son, that whoever believes in him should not perish but have eternal life."* The stories in the Bible show God's never-ending love and how he desires a relationship with each of us. God continually calls to us. Now is the time to begin your journey through the Bible.

What do you think?

1. What are some Bible stories you are already familiar with?
2. What is your favorite story in the Bible?
3. How do you show God that you love him?

SO GOD CREATED MAN IN HIS OWN IMAGE ... MALE AND FEMALE HE CREATED THEM.

—Genesis 1:27

Chapter Two

God Creates Our First Parents

Genesis

The story of salvation begins before time, as God creates everything out of love. In the Early World, Adam and Eve, our first parents, were created as one holy couple. When Adam and Eve sinned by disobeying God, our relationship with God was broken. But God's love for Adam and Eve, and for all of us, is so great that he offers his mercy and a promise of salvation. God's salvation will come to us through Jesus, a descendant of Adam and Eve. God will always love us, and he invites us to love him in return.

Bible Reading Checklist

- [ ] **GENESIS 1 The creation of the world**
- [ ] **GENESIS 2 God creates people and angels; God creates the Sabbath; God creates Adam and Eve**
- [ ] **GENESIS 3 The fall of Adam and Eve; God plans to save his creation**

The Creation of the World

Genesis 1:1–25

God has always existed. God is three equal Persons who share one divine nature. Another name for God is "The Holy Trinity." The three persons in the Holy **Trinity** are the Father, the Son, and the Holy Spirit. God had no beginning, has always existed, and will be forever (see CCC 290-292). In his great creativity, God created time, and he made our world out of nothing (see CCC 338).

The book of Genesis begins with two stories of creation. Both stories show that everything God created is good and that he loves what he created. He will always take care of his creation. The first story describes Creation this way: *"In the beginning, God created the heavens and the earth."*

On the first day, God separated light from darkness. He said, *"Let there be light!"* and there was light. On the second day, he made the sky.

On the third day, God separated the land from the seas. On the fourth day, he put the sun, the moon, and the stars in the sky.

On the fifth day, he filled the seas with fish and the sky with birds. Then, on the sixth day, God created all the land animals.

God Creates People and Angels

Genesis 1:26

On the sixth day, God also created human beings. He created human beings in his own image and likeness, male and female. Notice that every time God created something, he said, "This is good." But when God created people, he said, "This is *very* good."

God also made angels, the "hosts of heaven" (see CCC 326-327, 332; Isaiah 45:12; Psalm 103:19-21; Luke 2:9-15). Angels are spirits who can talk to God and to people. They are special messengers who go wherever God sends them, from heaven to earth and back again.

THE FALLEN ANGEL

One angel decided that he wanted to be greater than God. He wanted everyone to worship him instead of God, so he was cast out of heaven and came down to earth. That angel's name was Lucifer, and he is also called the devil or Satan. He hates God, and he tries to get people to hate God as well. We will read soon about how he appeared as a serpent to the very first people God made. It is because of him that we, too, are often tempted to turn away from God. We do not have to be afraid because God promises to protect and strengthen us against these temptations (see CCC 391-392).

God Creates the Sabbath

Genesis 2:1-3

God worked for six days to create everything. Finally, on the seventh day, God rested. He blessed the day of rest and made it holy. We call this day the **Sabbath**. On that special day we worship God and rest in his work. God created everything, including you and me. He wants us to be here! God created the earth over a period of time. The Bible calls it the six days of Creation. In his great creativity, God made time, and he made our world out of nothing. A carpenter uses hammers and nails to build things out of wood. A painter uses a canvas and paintbrush to create beautiful pictures. But God didn't need any tools or ingredients to make the heavens and the earth. God spoke the words "Let there be," and everything came into being! God used his words to make the heavens and the earth (see CCC 102; John 1:1). His Word is powerful!

SABBATH

The seventh day of creation, when God rested. Catholics honor the sabbath on Sunday, "The Lord's Day."

COVENANT An agreement between God and one or more people

God Creates Adam and Eve

Genesis 2:4-25

In the second Creation story, after God created the heavens and earth, he made the first human being—a man named Adam. He formed Adam out of the dust of the earth. He "breathed" into him to make him come alive.

God said, "It is not good that the man should be alone; I will make a helper for him." When Adam was fast asleep, God took one of the ribs from Adam's side, and he formed the first woman out of it.

Adam saw her and said, "Finally there is someone like me!"

She was named Eve, and she became Adam's wife.

God made people to be more like him than anything else in the world. The two Creation stories show us that everything God created is good and that he loves what he created.

God made Adam and Eve in his image. All people are created, both body and soul, in God's image. God wants us to live forever with him in heaven. We are also special because we can know who God is. We can love him and obey him. God gives us free will, which means we can choose whether or not to love (see CCC 1704).

I believe in one God, the Father almighty,
maker of heaven and earth, of all things visible and invisible.
I believe in one Lord Jesus Christ,
the Only Begotten Son of God,
born of the Father before all ages ...

TRINITY

God the Father, the Son, and the Holy Spirit are three distinct Persons who possess in common one single divine nature.

The Fall of Adam and Eve

Genesis 3:1-7

God gave Adam and Eve a beautiful garden called Eden. God met with them and instructed them to take care of the garden and the animals. He gave them fruit to eat from every tree except one. That one was called the Tree of the Knowledge of Good and Evil.

Satan came into the garden in the form of a serpent, a large snakelike creature. The serpent came to Eve and tempted her. He asked, *"Did God say you cannot eat the fruit of any tree in this garden?"*

Eve answered, "We can eat from any tree except the one in the middle of the garden. If we eat from that one, we will die."

The serpent replied with a sinister lie: *"You won't die! God knows that if you eat of it your eyes will be opened and you will be like him, knowing good and evil."*

So Eve took the fruit, tasted it, and gave it to Adam, who also ate it. After they ate the fruit, their eyes were opened, and they were ashamed. They realized that they had disobeyed God and had "fallen" into sin.

God called to them, but they were afraid now, and they hid from him. This is how sin and death entered the world, because they disobeyed God. Their sin is called **original sin**.

THE FIRST COVENANT: ONE HOLY COUPLE

Adam and Eve are the first couple who are united in marriage. God makes a covenant to bless the world through their union. The day of rest on the Sabbath was given to Adam and Eve as a time to rest and spend time with God.

God's Plan to Save His Creation

Genesis 3:8-24

As a loving Father, God asked Adam and Eve, "What have you done?" Adam and Eve told him what had happened.

God punished the serpent. God said, "Because you have done this, you will crawl on your belly forever. One day a descendant of the woman will crush your head." This promise from God is the beginning of the good news that God would one day redeem people from sin.

As for Adam and Eve, God gave them animal skins to wear so they would not be naked. God designed a way for male and female to work with him to create babies so that within a woman's **womb** new life can begin. God taught Adam how to grow food for them to eat.

SACRAMENT OF MATRIMONY

A husband and wife are united to each other and become "one flesh." They receive God's grace to love each other.

Because of their sin, their bodies would grow old and die. God said, "You will return to the ground. You were made from dust, and you will return to dust."

There was another important tree in the Garden of Eden called the Tree of Life. After Adam and Eve sinned, God did not want them to eat from the Tree of Life. If they ate from that tree, they would live forever knowing good and evil. As an act of mercy, God made them leave the garden, and he put a fiery angel near the tree to guard it.

The good news is that God had a loving plan. His plan would make it possible for people to once again be able to live in his presence for eternity. God gave a promise (see Genesis 3:15) to our first parents, Adam and Eve, that someday one of their descendants would defeat the Serpent, Satan. That descendant, as we will see, is Jesus, the Savior of the world. It is Jesus who conquers sin and death to bring us all back to God the Father who created each one of us.

What do you think?

1. How do you keep the Sabbath day holy?
2. In what ways are Adam and Eve like us? In what ways are they different?
3. How do you know that God loves you by observing the world around you?

I ESTABLISH MY COVENANT WITH YOU ...
AND NEVER AGAIN SHALL THERE BE
A FLOOD TO DESTROY THE EARTH.

—Genesis 9:11

Chapter Three

God's Family Grows

Genesis

Bible Reading Checklist

- [ ] GENESIS 4 Cain and Abel
- [ ] GENESIS 6 God asks Noah to build an ark
- [ ] GENESIS 7-8:19 The Flood
- [ ] GENESIS 8:20–9:17 God's covenant with Noah
- [ ] GENESIS 11:1-9 The Tower of Babel

Cain and Abel

Genesis 4

After Adam and Eve left the Garden of Eden, they had children. Their first two sons were named Cain and Abel.

Cain, the older son, learned how to grow plants as a farmer. Abel, the younger, learned how to raise sheep and goats. God showed them how to bring sacrifices to an altar as a way to worship him.

One day, Abel brought God his best animal as a way to thank God for all he had given to Abel. Abel sacrificed a lamb that was very dear to him. His brother, Cain, on the other hand, did not give God his best, nor did he have a thankful heart when he made his offering.

God wasn't happy with Cain's offering. God said to Cain, "Why are you angry? If you do not try your best, you might fall into sin. You must try to do good."

But Cain did not listen to God. He was angry with God for liking Abel's offering more than his. Cain became so envious of his brother that he killed Abel out in the field.

As punishment, God sent Cain to wander the earth away from the LORD's presence. Cain's sin separated him from God and other people. Eventually, Cain and his wife wandered to a new place and built a city there. Sadly, the people who came to live there were wild and did selfish things.

Adam and Eve had more children, and one of their other sons was named Seth. He was a man who loved God and had many children and grandchildren. Seth's family followed God's ways, and eventually one of his descendants, Lamech, had a son named Noah. Much later, Jesus also descends from Seth's family line.

God Asks Noah to Build an Ark

Genesis 6

Noah was the most righteous man on earth in his day. A righteous person is one who is good and does what is right.

Noah lived in a time when there was a lot of evil and violence in the world. God was disappointed in the bad choices people were making. No one chose to follow God except Noah, his wife, and their three sons and their wives. God decided to send a flood to wash away the wickedness in the world.

God told Noah, "Build a giant boat, called an ark, with rooms in it for you to live in. Make places inside for animals from all over the world. The ark will keep you all safe when the flood comes." Then God said, "Take two of every kind of animal and bird onto the ark with you, one male and one female. This way you will all be protected from the waters of the flood."

Noah built the ark and did everything God told him to do. Then God sent the rain, and for forty days and nights, it poured!

The Flood

Genesis 7-8:19

The earth was flooded, and all those who had acted wickedly were washed away. The water stayed on the earth for a long time, but Noah and his family and all the animals were safe inside the ark.

Gradually the water level went down until the ark settled on top of a mountain called Ararat. Noah sent out a dove to fly over the earth, and it returned to Noah holding a small olive branch. This was a sign of dry land, which meant that Noah and his family could leave the ark and start new lives on the earth.

The great Flood reminds us of our own baptism because the water washes away the wickedness of original sin and offers a new beginning of goodness. The ark reminds us of the Church, where we can live in faithful obedience to God and know that he will protect us (see CCC 1219).

THE SECOND COVENANT: ONE HOLY FAMILY

Noah and his family obey God and are saved from the flood. God makes a covenant with Noah that he will never again flood the whole world, and Noah will love and obey God. The rainbow in the sky reminds us of this covenant.

God's Covenant with Noah

Genesis 8:20–9:17

God told Noah, "Go out of the ark now. Bring everyone with you. *Be fruitful and multiply to fill the earth again*" (Genesis 9:7).

After Noah and his family and the animals came out of the ark, they built an altar and made a sacrifice to God. They were thankful that God had saved them from the flood.

Then God blessed Noah and Noah's sons. And God put a rainbow in the sky and said, *"Never again shall a flood destroy the earth."* The rainbow is a sign of the covenant, or promise, that he would never again flood the whole earth.

The Tower of Babel

Genesis 11:1-9

After the great Flood, Noah's three sons and their wives had many more children and grandchildren. Soon there were many people in the world, and they all spoke the same language. But once again, people became selfish. They said, "Let's build a city with a tower reaching to the heavens." They didn't want to honor God; they wanted to make a name for themselves.

They started building, but God didn't want them to be so proud, so he confused their speech (see CCC 57). Now that they spoke different languages, they couldn't understand one another and couldn't finish building the city with the tower.

God scattered the people, and they settled in different places all over the earth. The tower became known as the Tower of Babel, because the word *babel* means "confused speech."

These stories from the Early World period show us that God continues to show us the way for salvation so that people can choose to follow him. God wants us to trust and obey him so that he can protect us and give us many wonderful blessings.

Abel's sacrifice was pleasing to God because Abel had a sincere and thankful heart. Noah's ark sheltered and protected the life and goodness that God had brought into the world. The Tower of Babel showed the weakness of people as they tried to make their own way to God. They wanted to build a tower that would stretch up to heaven, but they didn't realize that God has a better way to get to heaven. It is by trusting in God and following his Way, through Jesus Christ, that we will be satisfied.

What do you think?

1. In what way does God protect you?
2. What does it mean to have a thankful heart?
3. What would the world be like if God hadn't saved the animals?

PATRIARCHS: Part I

"I WILL MAKE OF YOU A GREAT NATION, AND I WILL BLESS YOU."

—Genesis 12:2

Chapter Four

God Chooses Abraham to Become the Father of Many

Genesis

God calls Abram to go forth, and Abram obeys. He is later called "Abraham" by God and becomes a patriarch, or father, of God's people. Abraham, his son Isaac, and Isaac's son Jacob are three important patriarchs who listen to God and love God. God makes a covenant with Abraham with three promises: God will give Abraham land and a royal dynasty, and he will bless the whole world through him. Through Abraham, God's people become One Holy Tribe.

Bible Reading Checklist

- [ ] GENESIS 12:1-9, 13:5-12, 14:17-20 God promises Abram land, descendants, and worldwide blessing
- [ ] GENESIS 15, 17:1-19 God makes a covenant with Abram
- [ ] GENESIS 18, 21:1-13 A son is promised to Abraham and Sarah; the birth of Isaac
- [ ] GENESIS 22:1-18 Abraham's faith is tested
- [ ] GENESIS 24 Isaac marries Rebekah

God Promises Abram Land, Descendants, and Worldwide Blessing

Genesis 12:1-9; 13:5-12; 14:17-20

Abram was the great, great, great, great, great, great, great (seven greats!) grandson of Noah's son Shem. Abram lived in a land called Ur.

One day, God told Abram, "Take your family, your animals, and all your belongings and move to a new land called **Canaan**." Canaan was far away. Then God made a wonderful promise to Abram. God promised first to show Abram a new land; second, to make Abram's name great through many descendants; and third, to bless all the families of the world through Abram. This three-part promise is important in the Bible story. It will be fulfilled in Jesus Christ.

Abram obeyed God. He took his wife, Sarai, and his nephew Lot and moved to Canaan. Abram and Sarai settled in a hilly area, and Lot's family settled outside of a town called Sodom.

At that time, there were many small kingdoms in the land, and they fought with each other. Lot's family members were taken as prisoners during one of the fights. When Abram heard that Lot's family had been captured, he and some of his men rescued them at night.

On the way home, Abram met a king named Melchizedek. He was the king of Salem, the place we now call **Jerusalem**. Melchizedek was a king of peace and a priest of God Most High. He brought out bread and wine and blessed Abram with them, saying, *"Blessed be Abram, and blessed be God Most High!"* Abram then gave him one-tenth of everything he owned.

COVENANT WITH ABRAHAM Land Promise, Kingdom Promise, Worldwide Blessing

God Makes a Covenant with Abram

Genesis 15; 17:1-19

When Abram was ninety-nine years old, God renewed his promise to reward him greatly. Abram wondered how that could be since he still had no children. So God took Abram outside and said, *"Look toward heaven, and number the stars, if you are able to number them. ... So shall your descendants be."*

Then God made a covenant with Abram promising that he would make him the father of many people. When God made this covenant with Abram, he said, *"No longer will you be called Abram, but your name shall be Abraham!" Abraham* means "father of many nations."

God also changed Sarai's name to Sarah, which means "princess." Abraham promised to dedicate all his children and descendants to God and to obey all of God's laws. All of the men and boys would be **circumcised** (dedicated to God) as a sign of this covenant.

THE THIRD COVENANT: ONE HOLY TRIBE

God made a covenant with Abram, promising him that he would have as many descendants as there are stars in the sky. Circumcision is a sign of this covenant with the Jewish people.

A Son Is Promised to Abraham and Sarah

Genesis 18

After God promised Abraham and Sarah a son, three visitors came to Abraham to announce it. Abraham recognized the Lord. When Sarah heard that she was to have a son, she laughed and said, "How can I have a son? I am too old!"

Then God said, *"Is anything too hard for the Lord? When I return next spring, Sarah will have a son."*

Then Abraham walked with the three visitors down toward Sodom, where his nephew Lot lived. On the way, God told Abraham, "The people in Sodom and Gomorrah have become very evil." Because of this, their cities would soon be destroyed.

Abraham thought about all the people living there and about Lot and his family. Abraham begged God, "Please save the city for the sake of the righteous people living there!"

God promised to save the city if he could find just ten people that obeyed God and lived good lives. Sadly, there were not any righteous people living there except for Lot and his family. Lot and his daughters escaped just before the cities were destroyed.

The Birth of Isaac

Genesis 21:1-13

Just as the three visitors had said, Abraham and Sarah gave birth to a son. They named him Isaac, which means "laughter." Sarah was happy and said, *"God has made laughter for me!"*

Abraham and Sarah loved their new baby. When Isaac was eight days old, they circumcised him as a covenant sign that he was dedicated to God. Isaac grew into a fine boy.

Abraham's Faith Is Tested

Genesis 22:1-18

God wanted to help Abraham strengthen his faith. God tested him by asking Abraham to bring Isaac up to the mountain of **Moriah** and offer him as a sacrifice. Abraham agreed to do it, and he sadly prepared to give up his beloved son. Father and son climbed the mountain together. "Father," Isaac asked, "Where is the lamb for the offering?"

Abraham replied, "God himself will provide the lamb." Then Abraham built an altar and laid Isaac upon it. He believed that even if he sacrificed his beloved son on the altar, God could raise him from the dead.

As Abraham lifted a knife into the air, an angel of the LORD said, *"Do not lay your hand on the boy!"* God saw that Abraham was willing to do what he had asked, no matter how difficult.

Greatly relieved, Abraham took Isaac off of the altar. Looking around, he saw a ram caught in the bushes. Abraham sacrificed the ram in place of his son. Then God reminded Abraham once again that because he trusted God and obeyed him, God would bless him. Abraham would have many grandchildren and great-grandchildren who would live in the land God gave them through his covenant. All the nations of the earth would be blessed through them.

Isaac Marries Rebekah

Genesis 24

When Isaac was grown, he was ready to get married. Abraham told his servant, "Go back to Haran to find a wife for my son, Isaac." Haran is in the country Abraham came from. It was a long way from Canaan.

Abraham's servant traveled to Haran and found a beautiful girl there named Rebekah. She and her family agreed to let Abraham's servant take her back to the land of Canaan. They blessed her, saying, *"Our sister, be the mother of thousands of ten thousands!"*

Then she went to Canaan to marry Isaac. Isaac was happy to marry Rebekah, and he loved her very much. Their marriage shows us that love is a decision. Isaac chose to love her by an act of his own free will. That is why a wedding Mass includes the exchange of vows in which the man and woman promise to love each other until death parts them (see CCC 1626-1628).

What do you think?

1. Why does God sometimes make us wait for things?
2. How do you trust God in your own life?
3. How would you feel if you had to move from your home?

PATRIARCHS: Part II

"I AM YOUR BROTHER, JOSEPH, WHOM YOU SOLD INTO EGYPT. AND NOW DO NOT BE DISTRESSED, OR ANGRY WITH YOURSELVES, FOR GOD SENT ME BEFORE YOU TO PRESERVE LIFE."

—Genesis 45:4-5

Chapter Five

God Blesses Isaac, Jacob, and Joseph

Genesis

Bible Reading Checklist

- ☐ GENESIS 25:19-34; 27; 28:1-19 Jacob tricks Esau; Jacob dreams of a ladder
- ☐ GENESIS 29–30:24 Jacob marries and has children
- ☐ GENESIS 32:22-32; 35:10-29 Jacob wrestles with God
- ☐ GENESIS 37; 39–41 Joseph in Egypt
- ☐ GENESIS 42–46:4; 49:1, 8-10 Joseph and his brothers

Jacob Tricks Esau

Genesis 25:19-34; 27

Isaac and Rebekah had a difficult time having a baby, much like Abraham and Sarah. Finally, they were blessed with twin boys.

Before their sons were born, Rebekah had an unusual dream. Rebekah said, "Isaac, I dreamed that our sons were grown up and that the older son served the younger son. How can this be?" She was confused because this was the opposite of the custom: At that time, the birthright of inheritance was always given to the oldest son.

Rebekah's dream did come true. The older son, Esau, became a skillful hunter and worked in the fields. He was close to his father, Isaac. Jacob, the younger son, was quiet and liked to stay near the tents. He was the favorite of his mother, Rebekah.

One day, Esau came home very hungry. Jacob was cooking some stew.

"Let me have something to eat, or I will die of hunger!" Esau demanded.

"I will trade this food for your birthright," answered Jacob.

If he received the birthright, Jacob would be considered the oldest. Jacob, not Esau, would lead the family after Isaac's death. And Jacob, not Esau, would receive a double portion of land and possessions as his inheritance.

Esau was so hungry that he quickly made the trade and eagerly ate the stew. They did not tell their father, Isaac, about the trade.

Many years later, Isaac was very old and could no longer see well. He was ready to die and called Esau to him. "Esau," he said, "make me a meal of wild game. When you bring it to me, I will give you my blessing, which is your birthright as my firstborn."

Rebekah heard this, and while Esau was out hunting, she helped Jacob trick his father. They wanted Isaac to believe that Jacob was Esau so that Isaac would give Jacob the birthright blessing. Jacob even covered his arms with animal skins to make them feel like Esau's hairy arms. Isaac was almost blind and didn't know that he had blessed Jacob instead of Esau!

When Esau returned from hunting, the trick was discovered. "Please bless me, too!" Esau begged his father, but Isaac told him he could only give one blessing.

Even though Esau had agreed to trade his birthright for the bowl of stew many years before, he was furious with Jacob. Rebekah warned Jacob to run away to her family's hometown of Haran. Rebekah was sad to see Jacob leave, but she hoped he would find a good wife and be safe. While he was on the way to Haran, Jacob stopped to sleep and had a wonderful dream.

ISRAELITE A descendant of the patriarch Jacob, who was also known as "Israel."

Jacob Dreams of a Ladder

Genesis 28:1-19

Jacob dreamed of an incredible ladder that started on the earth and reached all the way to heaven. Angels were walking up and down the ladder, and God stood at the top.

God spoke to Jacob in the dream, promising Jacob that he would bless him with many children. God said to Jacob, "I will always be with you and keep you safe in the land I gave to Abraham and Isaac."

When Jacob woke up, he built an altar there and named the place Bethel, which means "house of God."

TWELVE SONS OF JACOB (ISRAEL)

Reuben, Simeon, Levi, Judah, Zebulun, Issachar, Dan, Naphtali, Gad, Asher, Joseph, and Benjamin.

Jacob Marries and Has Children

Genesis 29–30:24

When Jacob arrived in Haran, he fell in love with a girl named Rachel. Rachel was the daughter of Jacob's Uncle Laban.

Jacob said to Laban, "I would like to marry your younger daughter, Rachel." Laban answered, "Yes, but only if you agree to work for me for seven years." Jacob agreed to this and served Laban well.

When the seven years were over, the wedding finally took place. When Jacob gently lifted the bridal veil from his new bride's face, he was shocked to see not Rachel but her older sister, Leah! Laban had tricked Jacob into marrying Leah, because it was the custom for the oldest daughter to marry first.

Jacob had to work another seven years to marry Rachel. At that time a man could have more than one wife. During the years that Jacob worked for Laban, he had several sons with Leah, but no children with Rachel. After many years, Rachel gave birth to a son named Joseph, and she and Jacob were very happy. After Joseph was born, Jacob packed up all his belongings and moved his wives and eleven sons back home to Canaan. Laban did not want them to go, but Jacob, Rachel, Leah, and all their children and helpers left in the night.

Jacob Wrestles With God

Genesis 32:22-32; 35:10-29

One night, on the way back to Canaan, Jacob met a man outside. The two of them started to wrestle with each other. They wrestled until morning. Just as Jacob was winning the wrestling match, the man touched him on the hip, and it went out of joint.

Thinking that the man was an angel of God, Jacob asked, "Please bless me!" The man said, "Jacob, from now on your name will be changed to Israel." *Israel* means "one who prevails with God." Then Jacob knew he had been wrestling with God.

God renewed with Jacob the three covenant promises he had made with Abraham and Isaac: land, a royal dynasty, and worldwide blessing.

Jacob continued his journey back to the land of Canaan. It was there that Jacob's twelfth son, Benjamin, was born of Rachel. Sadly, Rachel died during the birth, and she was buried in Bethlehem.

The twelve sons of Jacob were named Reuben, Simeon, Levi, Judah, Issachar, Zebulun, Dan, Gad, Asher, Naphtali, Joseph, and Benjamin. Their families would become the twelve large tribes of people called Israelites. They are called Israelites because they are the descendants of Jacob, whom God named Israel.

Joseph in Egypt

Genesis 37; 39–41

The years passed. Jacob loved his twelve sons very much. His favorite son was Joseph, the first son of Rachel. He gave Joseph a special decorated coat with sleeves, but when his brothers saw it, they became envious.

Joseph shared two unusual dreams with his family, revealing that one day his brothers would bow down to him as though he were a king. "Who does he think he is?! Does he think he is better than us?" his angry brothers said.

Joseph's ten older brothers plotted against him. They tore the beautiful coat from Joseph, threw him into a dank pit, and then sold him to a band of **Ishmaelite** traders. At home, they lied, saying, "Father, wild animals have killed Joseph. Look, here is his coat!"

Jacob was completely heartbroken. "My poor Joseph!" he cried. He tore his clothes because he was so upset that Joseph was gone.

Meanwhile, the Ishmaelite traders took Joseph to **Egypt** and sold him to a man named Potiphar. Potiphar worked for the pharaoh, the king of Egypt. Potiphar liked Joseph and let him work in his home. But Potiphar's wife got angry with Joseph and had him thrown into jail.

While he was in prison, Joseph prayed to God for strength and wisdom. Two other prisoners, a butler and a baker who had worked for the pharaoh, had troubling dreams one night. Joseph saw that they were upset and said to them, "Interpretation of dreams belongs to God. Tell me your dreams, and God will let me know what they mean."

Joseph explained their dreams correctly. When the butler was released from jail, Joseph urged him, "Please tell the pharaoh about me."

The butler forgot about Joseph's request for a long time. But two years later, the pharaoh had a confusing dream. The butler remembered Joseph and told the pharaoh about him, so Joseph was brought up from prison.

Joseph asked God to help him, and then he told the pharaoh what the dream meant. He explained, "There will be seven years when all of Egypt will grow more than enough food for everyone. After this there will be seven years of bad crops. Then we will not be able to grow enough grain to feed everyone." Joseph advised the pharaoh to store up the extra grain from the seven good years so that they would have enough food for the seven bad years of famine.

The pharaoh was so impressed with Joseph's wisdom that he made him the second highest ruler in all of Egypt! Only the pharaoh had more authority than Joseph.

Joseph and His Brothers

Genesis 42–46:4; 49:1, 8-10

When the seven bad years came, Joseph's brothers in Canaan ran out of food. They went to Egypt to buy some grain. Joseph was in charge of selling the grain, so they had to bow before Joseph and ask for his permission. They didn't recognize him, but Joseph knew right away that they were his brothers.

Joseph told his ten brothers, "Bring your youngest brother, Benjamin, with you the next time you come for grain."

When they came back with Benjamin, Joseph surprised them all by revealing, "I am your brother Joseph, whom you sold into Egypt!" He continued, "Do not be distressed. It was for the sake of saving lives that God sent me here." Joseph's brothers were very sorry for how they had treated Joseph, and they were glad that he forgave them.

When Joseph's father, Jacob, learned that he was alive in Egypt, Jacob was overjoyed. He moved his family and servants to Egypt. There they could be close to Joseph, who made sure they had enough to eat during the famine years.

Then Jacob became sick and realized that he was near the end of his life. He called his twelve sons to his bedside, and he blessed each of them. He blessed his fourth son, Judah, with a special blessing. Jacob said, "The scepter shall never depart from Judah." Indeed, a great ruler would come from the family of Judah—that is, Jesus.

When Jacob died, his sons buried him in the cave of Machpelah in the land of Canaan. This is where Abraham and Isaac were also buried. After that, Jacob's sons, their children, grandchildren, and great-grandchildren stayed in Egypt for about four hundred years.

What do you think?

1. Have you ever had a very strange dream?
2. What blessings has God given your family?
3. How do you live patiently with God's plans for your life?

AND MOSES SAID TO THE PEOPLE, 'REMEMBER THIS DAY, IN WHICH YOU CAME OUT FROM EGYPT, OUT OF THE HOUSE OF BONDAGE.'

—Exodus 13:3

Chapter Six

God Delivers the Israelites from Egyptian Slavery

Exodus

The Israelites, who were the descendants of Jacob, stayed in Egypt for nearly four hundred years after Jacob and his family moved there. During this time they became slaves to the Egyptians. Although the Israelites remembered God, they became used to living in Egypt. God called Moses to set the Israelites free from slavery so that they could worship only him.

Bible Reading Checklist

- [ ] EXODUS 1–2 The birth and adoption of Moses
- [ ] EXODUS 3-4:23 The burning bush
- [ ] EXODUS 5:1-13; Read one chapter from EXODUS 7–10; EXODUS 11–12:39 The ten plagues and the first Passover
- [ ] EXODUS 13:17–15:10 The crossing of the Red Sea
- [ ] EXODUS 16:1-18; 17:1-7 God provides manna and water

The Birth and Adoption of Moses

Exodus 1–2

The descendants of Jacob, called the **Israelites,** lived for many years in the land of Goshen in Egypt. Eventually a new pharaoh came to power who did not know Joseph or his large family, and he made the Israelites work as slaves.

The pharaoh did not want the community of Israelites to get bigger. He ordered that all the baby boys should be thrown into the Nile River. This was a terrible thing to do!

Jochebed was the mother of a baby boy. She came up with a plan to save him. Jochebed put her baby in a papyrus basket, woven like a little ark, and she placed it among the reeds on the riverbank. Her daughter, Miriam, the baby's sister, followed the basket as it floated along. As Miriam watched, the daughter of Pharaoh came to bathe in the river and found the basket.

The baby in the basket was crying. Pharaoh's daughter knew that the baby was one of the Israelites' children, but she wanted to adopt him. Miriam stepped forward and asked, "Shall I find someone to help you take care of the baby until he is older?" Pharaoh's daughter said, "Yes, go and find someone to nurse him for me." Miriam took him back to their mother, Jochebed. Jochebed raised Moses until he was old enough to live in Pharaoh's house. Then Pharaoh's daughter named him *Moses,* which means "I drew him out of the water."

Moses grew up in Pharaoh's household as an Egyptian prince. He soon learned about the harsh treatment of the Israelite slaves. One day he saw an Egyptian master beating a slave. He killed the Egyptian and hid the body in the sand. Afraid that Pharaoh would learn of his crime, Moses ran away from Egypt and stayed in the land of Midian. There he married a woman named Zipporah, daughter of a man named Jethro. Moses lived with Jethro and his family for about forty years and helped them tend their flocks of sheep.

YAHWEH

The letters YHWH represent the divine name of God revealed to Moses. It means "I AM WHO I AM." The writers of the Bible substituted "LORD" so they did not take the divine name in vain.

The Burning Bush

Exodus 3–4:23

Moses was tending flocks on Mount Horeb, which is also called **Mount Sinai**. He came upon a bush that was on fire, but it wasn't burning up.

God called to Moses from the bush, saying, *"I am the God of your father, the God of Abraham, the God of Isaac, the God of Jacob."* God told Moses that he had heard the cries of the Israelites in Egypt. He remembered his covenant. He wanted Moses to lead them out of slavery in Egypt.

"Moses," God said. "You will lead the Israelites out of Egypt into a land flowing with milk and honey."

Moses said, "But what if the Israelites don't believe that I should be their leader?"

God replied, "Tell them that the God of your fathers has sent you. **I AM WHO I AM.**"

Moses was afraid no one would believe him. Like all shepherds in his day, Moses carried a long, sturdy wooden rod, or staff. God told Moses to throw his staff on the ground, where it changed into a snake. When Moses touched it, it turned into a staff again. God told him to use this miraculous sign when he went to Pharaoh.

Moses was also afraid to speak, so God told him to take his brother Aaron with him.

The First Nine Plagues

Exodus 5:1-13; Exodus 7-10

Moses and Aaron went to Pharaoh and said, "The God of Israel says to let the people go for a three days' journey into the desert. They need to offer sacrifices to the LORD there."

But Pharaoh's heart was hard, so instead of letting them go, he gave the Israelites even more work. "Now you have to make the same number of bricks, but you also have to gather your own straw!" ordered Pharaoh.

Soon Moses and Aaron returned and told Pharaoh again, "The God of Israel says, 'Let my people go.'" They showed Pharaoh a sign from God. Aaron threw his staff down, and it changed into a snake. Pharaoh's magicians responded by throwing down their own staffs. Their staffs also changed into snakes, but Aaron's snake swallowed their snakes. Still Pharaoh remained stubborn, just as God had told Moses he would.

Since Pharaoh's heart was hard and he would not listen, God sent ten **plagues** upon Egypt. First, God turned the river

to blood, but the Egyptian magicians did the same, so Pharaoh would not listen to Moses and Aaron. Then God sent a swarm of frogs, but the Egyptian magicians made frogs appear, too.

Pharaoh told Moses that if God took the frogs away, Pharaoh would let the people go. But when God did take the frogs away, Pharaoh changed his mind and would not let the Israelites go.

The third plague was gnats, and the fourth was flies. The fifth plague was a pestilence, which made all the Egyptians' animals sick. The sixth plague was boils, which caused sores on the Egyptians' skin.

The seventh plague was hail, which destroyed many crops. The eighth plague was locusts, which ate what crops were left. The ninth plague was three days of darkness. Through each of these signs from God, Pharaoh remained stubborn and would not let the Israelites go.

The Tenth Plague and The First Passover

Exodus 11-12:39

God brought one more plague upon the Egyptians. The tenth plague caused the death of all the firstborn in the land of Egypt.

God told the Israelites that their children would be saved if they sacrificed a lamb and used its blood to mark their doorposts. God also told the Israelites to ask their Egyptian neighbors for silver and gold.

That night, the Israelites ate lamb with unleavened bread and bitter herbs, as God told them to do, for they needed to be ready to leave Egypt quickly.

Every firstborn son in Egypt died that night, but the Israelites were saved by the blood of the lamb on their doorposts. This was the first Passover, for God had told them, *"When I see the blood, I will pass over you."*

Pharaoh's son died that night. In great sorrow, he at last let the Israelites go. They quickly gathered their belongings and left Egypt behind.

The Crossing of the Red Sea

Exodus 13:17–15:10

Almost immediately, Pharaoh changed his mind again. He commanded his army, "Go after the Israelites and bring them back!" Pharoah and his army chased the Israelites toward the Red Sea.

When the Israelites were at the water's edge, God said to Moses, "Lift up your staff and divide the water so that the people of Israel can walk across on dry ground." When Moses did this, the water split in two, and the Israelites walked between the two walls of water on dry land.

The Egyptians were in fierce pursuit, chasing after them, but the Israelites safely reached the other side. Then God told Moses to stretch out his hand over the sea, and the water thundered as it closed over the Egyptians.

God had saved the Israelites from slavery in Egypt! The Israelites celebrated with singing and dancing. They cried, *"The Lord is my strength and my song!"* This great deliverance from slavery was to be remembered year after year.

God Provides Manna and Water

Exodus 16:1-18; 17:1-7

After a short time in the desert, the Israelites began complaining to Moses about being hungry. Moses asked God what to do.

God told Moses, "I will give you meat to eat at night and bread from heaven in the mornings. Then you will know that I am the Lord your God."

The next morning, the Israelites gathered fine flakes of bread, called **manna**, which came from heaven and tasted like honey. In the evening, God sent them quail to eat.

The Israelites complained again and said they were thirsty. Again, Moses asked God what to do. God told Moses to take his staff and strike a rock. As soon as he hit the rock, water flowed out for the people to drink.

God had indeed kept his covenant with his people. He freed them from slavery, protected them from death, and gave them food and water so that they could live while they were in the desert.

What do you think?

1. What would it be like if your family was not allowed to go to Mass?
2. How would you feel crossing on the dry land between two giant walls of water?
3. What food does God provide us with at Mass?
4. What does it mean to listen to God's call?

"ALL THAT THE LORD HAS SPOKEN WE WILL DO, AND WE WILL BE OBEDIENT."

—Exodus 24:7

Chapter Seven

God Forms the Israelite Nation

Exodus

"Exodus" refers to the departure of the Israelites from Egypt. In their years in the desert, God formed the twelve tribes of Israel into a nation. God gave them the Ten Commandments as laws, and he gave them a place to worship him. This is where God told Moses how to anoint priests from the tribe of Levi. The priests would offer sacrifices on behalf of the people. God was taking good care of them.

Bible Reading Checklist

- [ ] EXODUS 19 The Israelites hear God at Mount Sinai
- [ ] EXODUS 20, 24:1-8 The Ten Commandments
- [ ] EXODUS 24:9–25:22; 31:7-11 Moses on Mount Sinai
- [ ] EXODUS 32; 34:1-9, 29-35 The golden calf
- [ ] EXODUS 40 Moses sets up the Tabernacle

The Israelites Hear God at Mount Sinai

Exodus 19

The Israelites walked in the wilderness until they came to a place called Sinai. There they set up their tents and waited while Moses went up the mountain.

The Lord spoke to Moses and said, "If you obey me, you will be my people."

The people stayed at the bottom of the mountain while Moses spoke with God. When they looked up at the mountain, it was covered with smoke. The mountain was shaking and thundering. The people knew God was there, and they trembled in awe of the Lord.

Moses came back to the people and told them what God had said. They agreed, *"We will do all that the Lord has spoken."*

The Ten Commandments

Exodus 20, 24:1-8

Moses returned to the mountaintop. God spoke to him and gave him ten laws, which we call the Ten Commandments. The commandments tell people how to live good lives by loving God and each other.

God had set the people free from slavery in Egypt. Now he was showing them how to avoid becoming slaves to sin and how to grow in their love for God (Deuteronomy 5:6-21; CCC 2052). These laws are for us, too.

The first three commandments show us how to love God.

The next seven commandments show us how to love one another.

When Moses came down from the mountain, he wrote down everything God had said to him. He said to the Israelites, "You have seen that God has talked with me from heaven." Then he read the book of the covenant to the people.

The people said, "We will be obedient." Then Moses sacrificed young bulls and sprinkled some of the blood on the people saying, *"Behold the blood of the covenant which the Lord has made with you."*

God promised to make the Israelites into a mighty nation of priests. The people agreed to obey the Ten Commandments and all the other laws.

THE TEN COMMANDMENTS

1. I am the Lord your God; you shall not have strange gods before me.
2. You shall not take the name of the Lord your God in vain.
3. Remember to keep holy the Lord's Day.
4. Honor your father and your mother.
5. You shall not kill.
6. You shall not commit adultery.
7. You shall not steal.
8. You shall not bear false witness against your neighbor.
9. You shall not covet your neighbor's wife.
10. You shall not covet your neighbor's goods.

THE FOURTH COVENANT: ONE HOLY NATION

God makes this covenant with Moses as he promises to make them a mighty nation of priests. The Ten Commandments are the sign of this covenant to which the Israelites respond, "All that the Lord has spoken we will do, and we will be obedient."

Moses on Mount Sinai

Exodus 24:9-25:22; 31:7-11

Then the Lord said, "Moses, come up on the mountain, and I will give you tablets of stone with the ten commandments written on them."

Moses and his helper, Joshua, went back up the mountain. When God returned, a cloud covered the mountain. God gave Moses instructions for building a **Tabernacle**, a dwelling place for God, saying, "The people shall make an ark from the materials they have brought from Egypt. I will tell you how to build it and how the priests should conduct worship."

Moses stayed on the mountain for forty days then left with the two stone tablets. God himself had written the Ten Commandments on those tablets for the people of Israel.

The Golden Calf

Exodus 32; 34:1-9, 29-35

Because Moses was gone so long, trouble began brewing at the bottom of Mount Sinai. The Israelites went to Aaron and grumbled, "We don't know what has happened to Moses. Make a god for us to worship!" Making a false god breaks one of the first commandments!

Unfortunately, Aaron agreed to help them. He instructed the people, "Bring all your gold jewelry, and we will melt it down." The people did this and used the molten gold to make a golden calf! They worshiped this idol instead of God.

When Moses and Joshua came down from the mountain, they heard shouting and singing, and they saw all the people dancing around the golden calf. Moses was so angry that he threw the two tablets with the Ten Commandments on the ground and broke them. Then he threw the golden calf into the hot fire. He punished the people for disobeying God.

Moses called out, "Whoever is for the LORD, come to me!" The men from the tribe of Levi came to Moses. They knew it was wrong to worship anything but God. Therefore, from that time on, only men from the tribe of Levi could become priests, because they had stayed faithful to God.

Moses loved the people even though they had sinned. He prayed for them, saying to God, "Remember Abraham, Isaac, and your servant Jacob whom you called Israel! Have mercy on the people to whom you promised descendants and land."

God listened to Moses and forgave the people. God promised to go with them as they traveled across the desert. Then the LORD told Moses, "Cut two more stone tablets so that I can write the ten commandments again to replace the tablets that were broken." This restored the covenant between God and his people. Moses took the tablets and went back up Mount Sinai, where he stayed for forty more days. When he came down again, his face was shining and radiant because he had talked with God!

Moses Sets Up the Tabernacle

Exodus 40

The Lord said to Moses, “On the first day of the first month, create the Tabernacle for a place of worship.” Moses gave the people the plans God had given him for building the Tabernacle. These instructions and other laws are written in the book of Leviticus.

Everyone worked carefully to make everything exactly as God wanted it. They made the tent, the tables, and the altars. They put up the lamps and sewed the clothing for the priests. They built the **Ark of the Covenant** to hold the tablets of the Ten Commandments and some manna from the desert. The Ark was a beautiful large box covered with gold and decorated with statues of two angels, also made of gold.

Moses said to Aaron, "God wants me to clothe you with the sacred vestments. He told me to anoint you and your sons as his priests!" Aaron and his sons came forward and were anointed as priests because they were from the tribe of Levi.

When everything was prepared, Moses set up the Tabernacle. He placed everything inside, just as God had told him. He offered sacrifices to God in front of the entrance. Moses and Aaron and his sons washed their hands and feet in the large bowl called a laver each time they went into the meeting tent or approached the altar of sacrifice. This meant that they were approaching God, who is holy, while remembering their own need of cleansing.

THE ARK OF THE COVENANT

God was present in the Tabernacle made by Moses and the Israelites. Catholics recognize God's presence in the tabernacle in the church where the Eucharist is kept.

To show Moses and the Israelites that God's presence was with them, a cloud covered the meeting tent and the glory of the Lord filled the Tabernacle.

The Israelites would camp in one location until the cloud rose. Then they would pack up all their tents and the Tabernacle, and they would travel on through the wilderness. In the daytime, they followed the cloud, and at night, there was fire in the cloud to light the way.

This is how the whole nation of Israel, One Holy Nation, followed God as he led them through the desert. God continued to feed them with manna every day.

HOLY WATER

Catholic churches have holy water fonts at their entrances to remind people of their baptism so that they might approach the sanctuary with a clean heart.

What do you think?

1. Why do we need to follow the same commandments today that God gave to Moses?
2. In what places do you feel that you are in the presence of God?
3. What happens when we do not obey God?

"THE LORD BLESS YOU AND KEEP YOU."

—Numbers 6:24

Chapter Eight

The Israelites Follow God in the Desert

Numbers

The book of Numbers tells the stories of the years the Israelites spent wandering in the desert after leaving Egypt. Moses obeyed God's command to number, or count, the people of Israel. The Israelites traveled through the desert for forty years as they struggled to trust in God alone.

Bible Reading Checklist

- [ ] **NUMBERS 1:1-3, 47-54; 3:1-4; 6:22-27** Numbering of the Israelites and Aaron's blessing
- [ ] **NUMBERS 11:1-10; 13** The Israelites complain; twelve scouts are sent to Canaan
- [ ] **NUMBERS 14** Failure to trust God leads to forty years of wandering
- [ ] **NUMBERS 17** Aaron's budding rod
- [ ] **NUMBERS 20:1-13; 27:12-23** Moses strikes the rock twice; God chooses Joshua

Optional: NUMBERS 22–24 Balaam and the donkey

Numbering of the Israelites and Aaron's Blessing

Numbers 1:1-3, 47-54; 3:1-4; 6:22-27

When the Israelites were ready to leave Mount Sinai, God asked Moses to count the people. They were going to the **Promised Land** of Canaan and would settle in twelve areas.

Moses gathered the twelve tribes of Israel to count them: Reuben, Simeon, Judah, Issachar, Zebulun, Ephraim, Manasseh, Benjamin, Dan, Asher, Gad, and Naphtali. These tribes were the descendants of Jacob's twelve sons. The tribe of Levi was not counted among the twelve because they were the priestly tribe, while Joseph's descendants formed two tribes, Ephraim and Manasseh, named for Joseph's two sons. The priests of the tribe of Levi would live among the other tribes in certain cities. While the other tribes had armies, the Levites had the duty to take care of the holy vessels of God in the Tabernacle. These vessels were the bowls, cups, lamps, and other items used to worship God.

God gave Moses and Aaron a special blessing to say over the Israelites:

> *"The LORD bless you and keep you!*
> *The LORD make his face to shine upon you, and be gracious to you!*
> *The LORD lift up his countenance upon you, and give you peace!"*
> *– Numbers 6:24-26*

As the Israelites traveled, the LORD went ahead of them with a column of cloud by day or a column of fire by night. God continued to provide manna as food for the people to gather each morning. By these signs, the LORD never left the Israelites.

The Israelites Complain

Numbers 11:1-10

In spite of all of God's gifts, the Israelites complained and grumbled. They said, "We wish we were back in Egypt! At least we had meat and fish and onions and garlic to eat!"

They were tired of wandering in the desert. They said, "Our strength is gone, and all we have to look at is this manna!"

They had quickly forgotten about God's many blessings. Their complaining made the journey through the desert more difficult.

Twelve Scouts Are Sent to Canaan

Numbers 13

Finally, the Israelites reached the land of Canaan, the Promised Land. The Lord told Moses to send twelve scouts, or spies, to survey the land and come back in forty days.

When they returned, the scouts reported that the land was *"flowing with milk and honey,"* just as God had promised. They brought back large grapes and figs that grew there.

Ten of the scouts were afraid of the people living in the Promised Land and said they were fierce giants who could not be overcome. The other two scouts encouraged the people to trust in God. The two scouts were Caleb from the tribe of Judah and Joshua from the tribe of Ephraim. Caleb and Joshua said, "If the Lord is happy with us, he will bring us into this land as he promised."

Failure to Trust God Leads to Forty Years of Wandering

Numbers 14

The Israelites believed the negative report of the ten scouts. They did not believe Caleb and Joshua. They cried out in despair saying, "Let's choose a leader to take us back to Egypt."

God wanted them to believe in his promise. He was sad that they forgot how he had blessed them. To teach the Israelites to trust him, God let them wander in the desert for forty years. During those years, the adults would grow old and die, but their children would live to enter the Promised Land. The two scouts, Caleb and Joshua, would also enter the Promised Land because they had trusted in God.

Aaron's Budding Rod

Numbers 17

While they were in the desert, the Israelites began to wonder whether God had really wanted Moses and Aaron to be their leaders. Some of them were jealous because only the Levites could be priests. They said, "Moses, you have gone too far! Why do you exalt yourself over us?"

Moses asked God for an answer. God told Moses to ask the Israelites for a wooden rod from each tribe. They wrote the name of the tribe's leader on each rod. For example, Aaron's name was on the rod for the tribe of Levi.

God said that one of the rods would sprout buds overnight. That rod would show which tribe God chose to lead the Israelites. So they put the rods in the meeting tent and left them overnight.

Moses said, "God will show us who he chooses to be the leader." In the morning, Aaron's rod had not only sprouted but also blossomed with ripe almonds! Aaron and the Levites were clearly the ones God chose to lead the Israelites. Aaron's rod was placed in the Ark of the Covenant along with the tablets of the Ten Commandments and a bowl of manna (see Hebrews 9:4).

Moses Strikes the Rock Twice

Numbers 20:1-13

As they continued traveling in the desert, the Israelites ran out of water, so the people began to complain to Moses. They demanded that he give them something to drink, saying, "Why have you made us come up from Egypt, to bring us to this evil place?"

Moses and Aaron asked God what they should do. The LORD told them to take the staff and go near the rock in front of the people. God said," Speak to the rock and command the water to flow from it."

So Moses and Aaron took the staff and went out to the people. However, when they gathered in front of the rock, Moses lifted the staff and struck the rock twice. This broke the crust that held the water, and the water flowed out.

Moses and Aaron had disobeyed God. God had said they should speak to the rock, because this was how he would show them they could trust him. Instead, they struck it. Because they had disobeyed God, neither Aaron nor Moses would live long enough to enter the Promised Land.

God Chooses Joshua

Numbers 27:12-23

During their forty years in the desert, a new generation grew up to enter the Promised Land. Aaron and his sister Miriam died and were buried.

Before Moses died, the LORD invited him to climb Mount Nebo so that he could see the Promised Land. Then God told Moses to appoint Joshua as the new leader of the Israelites.

Moses told the people, "I am 120 years old now, and I cannot go with you into the Promised Land. Joshua will be your leader. *Be strong and of good courage!*" (Deuteronomy 31:7).

Joshua stood in the presence of the priest Eleazar, son of Aaron, and the whole community. Then Moses laid his hands on him and commissioned him to take the Israelites into the Promised Land. Joshua was now the leader of the Israelites.

Balaam and the Donkey

Numbers 22–24

The Israelites moved on and camped on the plains of Moab. They were right across from the Promised Land of Canaan.

Balak, the King of the Moabites, was afraid of the Israelites because they were a strong nation. King Balak asked a prophet named Balaam to curse the Israelites so that they would lose to the Moabites in battle. However, God told Balaam, "The Israelites are blessed, so you cannot curse them!"

Balaam told Balak, but Balak tried a second time. He sent princes to Balaam to bring him to Balak to curse the Israelites. Balaam said, "I can only do what the LORD tells me to do," but he agreed to go with the princes. They rode on donkeys to Balak.

On the way, an angel of the LORD appeared on the road to stop Balaam. The donkey that Balaam was riding on saw the angel and turned off the road. Balaam could not see the angel, so he beat his donkey to try to make him go on ahead. But the donkey would not budge.

After the third try, God allowed the donkey to talk, and the donkey said, "What have I done to you that you should beat me these three times?" Balaam told the donkey, "You have acted stubbornly against me."

Then the LORD allowed Balaam to see the angel standing on the road, and Balaam fell to his knees. He knew that his donkey was trying to obey God and that he should, too.

When Balaam reached King Balak, Balaam did not curse the Israelites. He blessed them. Balak tried three times to get Balaam to curse the Israelites, but each time Balaam blessed them instead.

What do you think?

1. When have you gotten a chance to do something over?
2. Tell about a time you were chosen to do an important job.
3. Why do we sometimes grumble about life in spite of God's goodness?

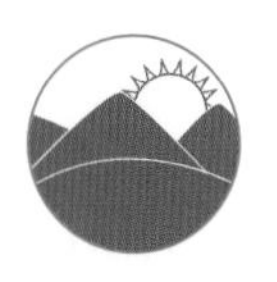

BE STRONG AND OF GOOD COURAGE ... FOR THE LORD YOUR GOD IS WITH YOU WHEREVER YOU GO.

—Joshua 1:9

Chapter Nine

The Israelites Enter the Promised Land

Joshua

After Moses died, God chose Joshua to lead the Israelites into the land of Canaan The conquest of the armies they face is made possible by Joshua's trust in God. In this way God fulfills the first of his three promises to Abram: The Israelites settle in the Promised Land.

Bible Reading Checklist

- [ ] **JOSHUA 1** Joshua, Israel's new leader
- [ ] **JOSHUA 2** Rahab hides the spies
- [ ] **JOSHUA 3-4** Israel crosses the Jordan
- [ ] **JOSHUA 6, 10:1-15** The fall of Jericho; the sun stands still
- [ ] **JOSHUA 21:41-45, 24:1-28** Covenant renewal

Joshua, Israel's New Leader

Joshua 1

God promised Joshua that he would stay with him wherever he went. He told Joshua to be strong and brave and to obey all the laws that Moses gave them. That way, Joshua and all of God's people would be successful in the land of Canaan, the Promised Land. God said they should study the law every day and do everything that is written in it.

Once again, God told Joshua, "Be strong and filled with courage." God said, "Cross over the Jordan River with all of the Israelites and enter the land that I have promised the people of Israel."

So Joshua told the people what God said and asked them to get ready to move. He told them what to pack and when they would go. The people told Joshua, "We will obey you and do what God commands." They would follow Joshua as they had followed Moses before him.

Rahab Hides the Spies

Joshua 2

Joshua sent two of his men ahead into the land. He told them to secretly learn what they could about the city of Jericho.

The men went out and spied on the city. They had to be very careful, because the king of Jericho didn't want them to come. He did not want the Israelites to live there.

The two spies went to the house of a woman named Rahab, and she was kind to them. She told them that the people of Jericho were afraid of the Israelites and their powerful God. When she heard that the king wanted to arrest the men, she hid them on the roof of her house so they could escape.

Rahab trusted God, and she knew that the spies were from the people of God. She said, "Please save my family from the coming battle."

The two spies promised Rahab that she and all her family would be safe in the battle of Jericho. They said, "Tie a bright red cord in your window as a signal for the soldiers. That way they will know who to save."

Then the two men went back to Joshua and told him that the people in Jericho were afraid of the Israelites and that God would help them win.

Israel Crosses the Jordan

Joshua 3–4

The priests, carrying the Ark of the Covenant, led the Israelites down to the Jordan River. When the priests stepped into the water, it stopped flowing and piled up on one side, leaving a dry path. So, the people crossed the Jordan safely and entered the Promised Land.

Twelve men each took a large stone out of the river. Joshua set them in a pile as a memorial. In the future, when children would ask their fathers, "What do these stones mean?" their fathers would tell them, "Israel crossed over the Jordan on dry ground." This event reminded them of the Exodus, when God had caused the Red Sea to part so that the Israelites could escape from the Egyptians.

The Fall of Jericho

Joshua 6

The city of Jericho was surrounded by a high, strong wall. God told Joshua how the Israelites should get into the city. The priests carried the Ark of the Covenant out in front of all the Israelites. They marched around the outside wall of the city once a day for six days. Then, on the seventh day, they marched around the city seven times.

During the last march around the city, the priests blew on trumpets and all the people shouted. Amazingly, the wall around the city fell down so that all the Israelites could go in. The spies saw the bright red cord that Rahab had hung from her window. They saved her and her family because she had helped the Israelites.

After the battle, Rahab married an Israelite named Salmon, of the tribe of Judah. She became the great-great-grandmother of King David and one of Jesus' ancestors.

The Sun Stands Still

Joshua 10:1-15

Soon after the battle of Jericho, the people from the town of Gibeon made an alliance with the Israelites. This meant that they would be friends, live in the same land, and protect each other. However, when five neighboring Amorite kingdoms heard about the alliance, they became afraid. They decided to band together to attack Gibeon. Joshua's men came back to camp and said, "The people of Gibeon are in trouble because the Amorites are trying to kill them."

Joshua prayed. God told him to be courageous because God was with him and would give the Israelites victory. Joshua led a surprise attack, and God fought along with the Israelites, throwing great hailstones down from the sky on the enemy armies. Then God caused the sun and moon to stand still until Joshua and his men could rescue all the people in Gibeon.

The people praised God and thanked him for making the sun and moon stand still long enough for everyone to be saved.

Covenant Renewal

Joshua 21:41-45; 24:1-28

Joshua and the Israelites came into the Promised Land to inherit what God had promised them. The twelve tribes each settled into their own territories, which were named for the sons of Jacob: Naphtali, Issachar, Benjamin, Simeon, Asher, Zebulun, Gad, Dan, Reuben, and Judah—and for the two sons of Jacob's son Joseph: Ephraim and Manasseh. One tribe, the tribe of Levi, did not receive its own territory, because the Levites were designated as priests. Instead, they were given forty-eight cities to live in among the twelve territories.

There was peace in the land of Israel for many years after the settlement of the territories.

When Joshua was an old man, he became tired and sick. He called a meeting of all the leaders and judges of Israel and told them, "Keep all the laws of the Book of Moses, obey God, and be very brave." He reminded them of all the good things God had done for them and all the promises God had kept for them. He warned the people, "Do not worship other gods, but keep faithful to the one true God. Remember that God is faithful to you."

The people promised to obey God. To make it official, Joshua wrote down their agreement in the Book of the Law of God. Then he set up a memorial stone by the sanctuary where they kept the Ark of the Covenant. This would remind the people of their promise to obey God. Then the people all went back to their homes, and Joshua died peacefully at the age of 110.

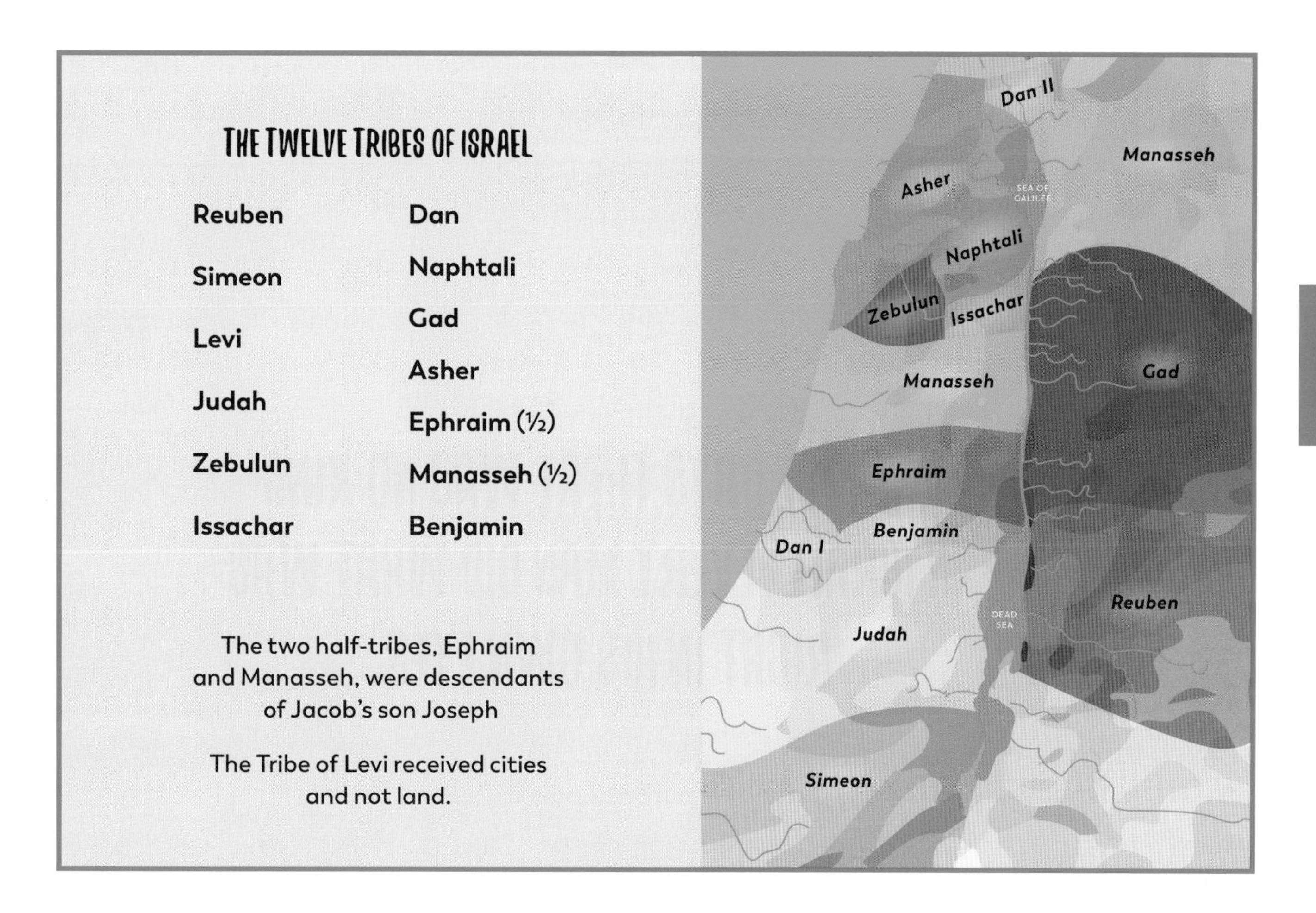

What do you think?

1. What are some of the responsibilities that your priest has?
2. Have you ever made a promise to God? Have you kept it?
3. How can we trust in God to work through us to accomplish his will?

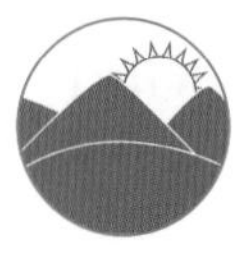

IN THOSE DAYS THERE WAS NO KING IN ISRAEL; EVERY MAN DID WHAT WAS RIGHT IN HIS OWN EYES.

—Judges 21:25

Chapter Ten

The Judges Lead the Israelite Tribes

Judges

After Joshua died, the Israelites found themselves without a leader. People decided to do what they thought was right instead of asking God to guide them. The result was chaos and defeat in battle. Twelve judges, one from each of the twelve tribes of Israel, took turns leading the Israelites. As each judge ruled them, the Israelites experienced a new cycle of struggle: after their sin, servitude (as they were conquered by enemies), supplication (as they prayed for relief), salvation (when God rescued them), and finally silence, when the people should have taught their children the ways of God but did not.

Bible Reading Checklist

- [ ] JUDGES 2 Israel is unfaithful to God's covenant
- [ ] JUDGES 4–5:5 Deborah the judge
- [ ] JUDGES 6–8:28 Gideon the judge
- [ ] JUDGES 13, 16, 21:25 Samson the judge
- [ ] RUTH 1–4 Ruth becomes part of the family of the Messiah

Israel Is Unfaithful to God's Covenant

Judges 2

The twelve tribes of Israel settled into the parts of the Promised Land allotted to them. God had told them to conquer the Canaanites, but instead of driving the Canaanites out, the Israelites lived among them. They shared the land and soon began to follow their ways.

The Israelites began to worship the false gods of the Canaanites. Some of the Israelites married people from Canaan. They forgot about their covenant with the God of Abraham, Isaac, and Jacob.

In the wilderness, the Tabernacle had been in the center of the Israelite camp. Now it was set up in a place called Shiloh. For most of the Israelites, Shiloh was a long distance to go to worship.

Seven times the Israelite tribes struggled with their enemies, and each time God sent leaders, called judges, to rescue them. The judges were brave leaders who led the Israelite tribes when their enemies attacked them. After God rescued them, the Israelite tribes would live peacefully for a while. But then the Israelite tribes would once again forget their covenant with God and return to worshiping the idols of the Canaanites.

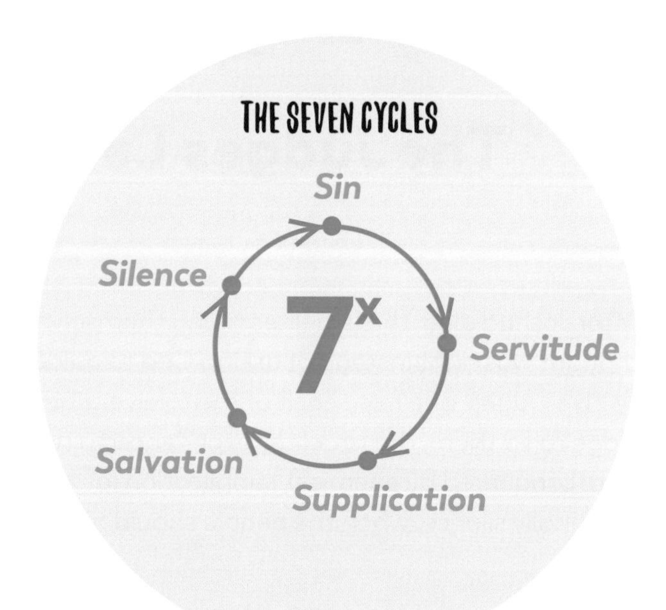

Deborah the Judge

Judges 4–5:5

One of the judges was a woman named Deborah, who would sit beneath a palm tree to give counsel. The Canaanite King Jabin captured the nearby Israelites and treated them cruelly for twenty years.

Deborah asked a man named Barak to go to the tribes of Naphtali and Zebulun to gather an army. Barak said, "If you go with me, I will go."

Deborah answered, "I will go with you."

So Barak brought ten thousand men to Mount Tabor and chased out the enemy army. The leader of the enemy army was named Sisera. Sisera ran away and hid in a tent, but a woman recognized him and put him to death. That is how, with Deborah leading them, the Israelites defeated the Canaanite king Jabin and lived again in peace.

Gideon the Judge

Judges 6–8:28

There were forty years of peace in the land. During this time, the Israelites began sinning against God again. Because of this, the Midianites were able to rule over them for seven years. When they cried out in **repentance** and supplication to the Lord, God heard their cry. He agreed to save the Israelites through another judge named Gideon.

Gideon was the youngest member of an unimportant family in the tribe of Manasseh, and he was unsure of God's call. To test God, he put a fleece (or sheepskin) onto the ground and said, "If in

the morning the dew is only on the fleece and the ground is dry, then I know that I should lead the Israelites."

The next morning the ground was dry and the fleece was full of water. But Gideon was still unsure and asked for another sign—this time, a dry fleece on the wet ground. The next morning, the ground was wet, but the fleece was dry. Now Gideon trusted in the LORD and prepared to answer his call.

Gideon looked for men to help him fight the huge Midianite army. He chose a small army of only three hundred men. God told him to choose those who drank from a stream by lapping water from their hands. God wanted to show that they could defeat a large army with his help.

Gideon gave each soldier a clay jar with a torch inside and a horn. When darkness came, the small army surrounded the Midianite camp. Then all together they smashed their pots, waved their torches, and blew on their horns to make lots of noise.

The Midianites were terrified and ran away because they thought a huge army was attacking them. Gideon's little army had won the battle!

After the Israelite victory over Midian, there was peace for another forty years.

Samson the Judge

Judges 13, 16, 21:25

After a time of peace, the Philistines began to fight with the Israelites. God sent Samson as the judge to save the Israelites from this new enemy.

Samson was a gift to his parents because they had not had children for many years. They raised him with the special vow of a **Nazirite**. Part of the vow was to never cut his hair.

Samson, whose name means "sunshine," grew to be one of the strongest men around. He fought many battles against the Philistines. Unfortunately, Samson fell in love with a Philistine woman named Delilah. Her name means "nighttime." The leaders of the Philistines told Delilah, "We need to know what makes Samson so strong. We will pay you to find out the secret of Samson's strength." They wanted to throw him in prison.

Selfishly, Delilah agreed to the plan. Several times she said to Samson, "Tell me the secret of your strength."

Samson said, "I will become weak if I am tied up with seven fresh bowstrings," so Delilah tied the strings around him to test him. Then she yelled, "Samson! The Philistines are upon you!" But Samson broke the bonds easily.

Twice more Delilah asked Samson what would make him weak, but each time she tried to tie him down, he broke free. Then Delilah complained and pouted until Samson was tired of hearing her whine. He told her the truth, saying, "I have been consecrated to God, and no razor has ever cut my hair." After he fell asleep that night, Delilah ran out and told the leaders of the Philistines to come. As Samson lay sleeping on her lap, a Philistine cut his hair. When Delilah yelled that the Philistines were upon him this time, Samson couldn't escape, because his strength was gone. The Philistines poked out his eyes and took him to prison.

Samson was in prison for a long time. He was sorry that he had broken his vow to God and asked God to forgive him.

The leaders of the Philistines assembled to thank their false god, Dagon, for delivering Samson to them. They brought Samson into their temple to make fun of him. They chained him between two columns.

Since Samson had been in prison so long, his hair had grown back, and his strength had returned. While he stood tied to the columns, he prayed, *"Lord God, remember me and strengthen me, I beg you!"* Then he pushed hard on the columns. The temple collapsed on him and everyone inside! In his death, Samson had the last victory over the Philistines!

TWELVE JUDGES

Othniel
Ehud
Shamgar
Deborah
Gideon
Tola
Jair
Jephthah
Ibzan
Elon
Abdon
Samson

Ruth Becomes Part of the Family of the Messiah

Ruth 1–4

During this time, there was a famine in the territory of Judah; there was no food to eat. A man named Elimelech and his wife, Naomi, moved from Bethlehem to the plains of Moab looking for food. The Moabites worshiped false gods, but Elimelech and Naomi found food and settled there.

Naomi's husband died, and her two sons married Moabite women named Orpah and Ruth. Sadly, both of Naomi's sons also died, leaving her alone in the strange land. She decided to return to her relatives in Bethlehem.

Orpah stayed in Moab, but Ruth went to Bethlehem with Naomi. Ruth chose to be faithful to Naomi and to God, telling her mother-in-law, "Your people shall be my people and your God my God."

In Bethlehem, Ruth met a man named Boaz, who was from the same family as Elimelech, her deceased father-in-law. Ruth took care of Naomi by working in Boaz's fields. When Boaz learned Ruth's story, he asked her to marry him.

Boaz, who was from the tribe of Judah, married Ruth, and they had a son named Obed, who had a son named Jesse. Jesse became the father of David, who would later become a king of Israel. Jesse is an important person in the family line of Jesus, the **Messiah**.

During the time of the judges, the Israelites did what was right in their own eyes. They had a hard time following God's laws in their new land. They did not have a strong leader like Moses or Joshua. God wanted to be their leader, but the Israelites were influenced by the culture around them and often forgot about God.

What do you think?

1. What in your own life distracts you from following God's law?
2. If you have sinned, what can you do to make yourself right with God again?
3. What makes a good leader?

"BEHOLD, TO OBEY IS BETTER THAN SACRIFICE."

—1 Samuel 15:22

Chapter Eleven

The Israelites Ask for a King

1 Samuel

In Canaan, God established Israel as a royal kingdom under David and promised him an eternal throne. The color purple represents the royal throne. God called Samuel to serve him when Samuel was still young. Samuel was a prophet who loved God and listened to him. When he was grown, Samuel led the Israelites to defeat the Philistines, and he governed them as their judge until he was old. God longed to be their one, true king, but the Israelites wanted a king like the kings in other nations. God allows a royal kingdom to be established with three major kings: Saul, David, and Solomon.

Bible Reading Checklist

- [ ] 1 SAMUEL 1-2:26; 3 Hannah asks God for a child; God calls Samuel
- [ ] 1 SAMUEL 4:1-11; 5:1-5; 7:1-6; 8 The Philistines Capture the Ark; Israel asks for a king
- [ ] 1 SAMUEL 9-10:1 Samuel anoints Saul as the first king of Israel
- [ ] 1 SAMUEL 15:10-26; 16 Saul disobeys God; Samuel anoints David to be king of Israel
- [ ] 1 SAMUEL 17-18:9; 31:1-6 David defeats Goliath; the death of King Saul

Hannah Asks God for a Child

1 Samuel 1–2:26

There was a man named Elkanah and his wife, Hannah. They went to the Tabernacle at Shiloh to bring offerings to the Lord.

Hannah began to cry while she prayed. She was very sad because she didn't have any children. She asked God to give her a son. She said, "If you give me a son, I will give him back to you. He will live in your presence and serve you."

Eli, the priest, saw her praying and asked her why she was so sad. When Hannah told him, Eli blessed her and said, "Go in peace; God will answer your request."

By the next year, Hannah's prayer was answered, and she had a baby boy. She named him Samuel.

When the boy was old enough, Hannah brought him to the Tabernacle to live there and help the priests. Hannah sang a song of praise and thanksgiving to God.

Later, God blessed Hannah and Elkanah with five more children. Hannah and Elkanah visited the Tabernacle every year. They brought Samuel a new linen robe to wear while he helped Eli, the priest.

God Calls Samuel

1 Samuel 3

Samuel learned many things from Eli as he grew up. One night while he was sleeping, Samuel heard someone call him: "Samuel! Samuel!" He thought it was Eli.

Samuel ran to Eli and said, "Here I am, for you called me." But Eli hadn't called Samuel, and he sent him back to bed.

This happened three times. Finally, Eli realized that it was God who was calling Samuel. Eli told Samuel to answer next time by saying, *"Speak, LORD, for your servant is listening."*

Samuel obeyed Eli and went back to bed. The LORD God called to Samuel again. This time Samuel answered, "Speak, LORD, for your servant is listening."

From then on, whenever God spoke to Samuel, Samuel listened carefully. Then he would tell the people what God had said. He became a faithful **prophet**.

The Philistines Capture the Ark

1 Samuel 4:1-11; 5:1-5; 7:1-2

The Philistines attacked the Israelites again. The elders of Israel thought it would be a good idea to bring the Ark of the Covenant into battle to help them win.

Instead, they lost the battle, and many Israelites were killed.

The Philistines captured the Ark and put it into one of their temples. The next morning, the idol of their false god Dagon had fallen on its face. It looked as if it were bowing before the Ark.

The Philistines became afraid of the Ark and said, "Send it away so that it won't slay us!" They passed it from city to city until they finally decided to send it back to Israel on an ox cart. The Ark of the Covenant ended up in the town of Kiriath-Jearim and stayed there for twenty years.

Israel Asks for a King

1 Samuel 7:3-6; 8

Samuel led the Israelites in another fight against the Philistines. The Israelites were afraid and asked Samuel to pray that God would deliver them. God threw the Philistines into confusion that day. The Israelites defeated them and gained back the lands the Philistines had taken from them.

For many years after that, the Israelites lived at peace, and Samuel was their leader and their judge.

When Samuel was old, the people began to turn away from God again. They told Samuel, "We want a king like all the other nations!" Samuel didn't want to appoint a king over Israel, because he believed God alone should be their king. He warned the people that a human king would make their lives hard. But God told Samuel, "They are rejecting me as their King. Give them a king."

Samuel Anoints Saul as the First King of Israel

1 Samuel 9–10:1

God told Samuel to find a man named Saul. Samuel anointed Saul's head with oil to show that Saul would become the king.

Saul was the first king of Israel. Samuel stayed with him for many years. He gave Saul advice about how to act as king.

There were many wars. Saul was a good military leader and protected the Israelites from the surrounding nations. Saul led well in the early years of his reign, but later he disobeyed God. He stopped listening to Samuel. Saul decided he would make a sacrifice on an altar instead of waiting for Samuel the priest to do it. God was displeased because Saul did not obey. Samuel said, "You have acted foolishly and have not obeyed God!" Therefore, God told Samuel to anoint another king to take Saul's place.

Saul Disobeys God

1 Samuel 15:10-26

Saul continued to disobey God. Samuel told Saul that God wanted him to punish Amalek and destroy everything in the nation. God asked for this because Amalek had not allowed the Israelites to pass through the land when they came from Egypt. Saul led his army in an attack against Amalek. But instead of destroying everything, Saul spared the best sheep, oxen, and lambs, keeping them for himself and his troops. God was disappointed that Saul had not obeyed him, and he sent Samuel to confront him. When Samuel met Saul, he heard the bleating of the sheep and the lowing of the oxen. Saul couldn't hide the animals he had taken. Samuel rebuked Saul, saying, "You rejected the request of the LORD, and now the LORD has rejected you as king of Israel."

Samuel Anoints David to Be King of Israel

1 Samuel 16

God told Samuel, "Go to Bethlehem to the house of a man named Jesse and find the boy David. Pour oil on his head to show that David will be the next king of Israel. David will replace Saul."

David was a young shepherd who played songs on his harp and cared for sheep in the fields. Samuel found him and did as God asked. God's Holy Spirit filled David that day.

After his anointing, but before he was declared the new king, David went to work for Saul. He became Saul's armor-bearer. David also played his harp for Saul to soothe the king when he was distressed.

David Defeats Goliath

1 Samuel 17-18:9

When David was still tending his father's sheep, his brothers followed Saul into battle against the Philistines in the Elah Valley. One day, David brought food to his brothers on the battlefield and watched an enormous Philistine named Goliath yell curses at the Israelites and against God. "Let one of you come out and fight me," shouted Goliath. "Whoever wins will be the winner of this battle."

As a shepherd, David had killed lions and bears to protect his father's sheep. So David went to King Saul and told him that he wanted to fight the giant. David said, "God is with me, so I am not afraid."

Saul gave David permission to fight Goliath and gave him his armor to wear. When David put on the armor, however, it was so big and heavy that he couldn't even walk! David took off the armor and stayed in his regular clothes. He went to a brook to pick out five smooth stones to use in his sling. Then he went to the battleground.

When Goliath saw David, he laughed and said," Am I a dog that you hit with a stick? I will kill you!"

Goliath was big and strong, but David trusted God. David shouted, "This battle is the Lord's, and he will win!" Then David took a stone out of his pouch, placed it into the sling, and let it fly toward Goliath. The stone hit the giant squarely in the head, and he fell over dead. God had saved the Israelites through the faith of young David.

The Death of King Saul

1 Samuel 31:1-6

David became well known because of his heroic battle with Goliath, and the people loved him. King Saul's son Jonathan became David's best friend. But King Saul was jealous of David. In the years that followed, he watched David's every move and even tried to have him killed.

David spent many years running away from Saul's men and hiding in caves. Finally, there was a terrible battle with the Philistines on Mount Gilboa. Saul's sons were killed while fighting. Saul was also wounded in the battle. When he saw that his sons had been killed, he was so distressed that he fell on his sword and killed himself.

What do you think?

1. What would be a good time in your day to be quiet and listen for God's voice?
2. Did you ever ask for a gift thinking it would satisfy you forever?
   What happened to that gift?
3. What does it mean to obey God's law?

ROYAL KINGDOM: Part II

"AND YOUR HOUSE AND YOUR KINGDOM SHALL BE MADE SURE FOR EVER BEFORE ME; YOUR THRONE SHALL BE ESTABLISHED FOR EVER."

—2 Samuel 7:16

Chapter Twelve

God Builds a House Through David and Solomon

2 Samuel, 1 Kings

Each of the three kings in the Royal Kingdom contributed to the One Holy Kingdom of God in different ways. King Saul united the Kingdom of Israel as he fought many battles. Through King David, God fulfilled his promise to establish a royal dynasty. King David's son, Solomon, followed David as king and built a Temple as a new home for the Ark of the Covenant.

Bible Reading Checklist

- [ ] 2 SAMUEL 1:1-16; 2:1-10; 5:1-12 David becomes king of all Israel
- [ ] 2 SAMUEL 6-7:16 David brings the Ark to Jerusalem
- [ ] 2 SAMUEL 11–12:15 David sins and repents
- [ ] 1 KINGS 1:28-40; 3:1-15 Solomon is anointed king and asks for wisdom
- [ ] 1 KINGS 8:1-21; 9:1-9; 11:7-13 Solomon builds God's Temple

David Becomes King of All Israel

2 Samuel 1:1-16; 2:1-10; 5:1-12

David and all Israel mourned the death of their first king. After King Saul's death, the people of Judah anointed David king over all of Israel. He was thirty years old when he began his reign, and he reigned forty years. He was loved as a warrior and leader.

King David and his men captured Jerusalem and called it the City of David. He built a palace there and made Jerusalem the capital of all of Israel.

David Brings the Ark to Jerusalem

2 Samuel 6-7:16

David brought the Ark of the Covenant into Jerusalem with joyful singing and dancing. The procession was like a holy parade. David danced and all the people rejoiced. The presence of God was coming into their city!

David was happy. He wanted to build a great temple to house the Ark of the Covenant. He wanted God's house to be a beautiful building instead of a tent.

God told him, "I have moved with you wherever you went. I do not need a house. Instead, I will build a house for you." Then God made a covenant with David, his anointed king, to establish a royal dynasty. This would be known as the house of David.

At the beginning of salvation history, God made a covenant with Abraham, promising to make his name great and bless all the earth through his descendants (see Genesis 22:15-18). David was a descendant of Abraham. One of David's descendants would be God's own son, Jesus, the promised Messiah who would bring salvation to all the world.

THE FIFTH COVENANT: ONE HOLY KINGDOM

God promised that David's kingdom, *One Holy Kingdom*, would last forever and that he would not take his steadfast love away from him. The sign of this covenant is the Temple in Jerusalem, which was built by David's son Solomon.

David Sins and Repents

2 Samuel 11–12:15

David ruled as a good king for a long time. Once, however, while his armies were away fighting, David fell in love with another man's wife. Her name was Bathsheba. David took her into his palace and arranged to have her husband killed in battle.

David recognized the evil of his sins of murder and adultery. Deeply saddened, he repented with his whole heart. He was very sorry for what he had done and longed for a chance to be close to God again.

God knew that David's heart was changed, and God forgave David. David wrote many psalms in the Bible, including one that shows us his repentant heart. He prayed, *"Create in me a clean heart, O God, and put a new and right spirit within me"* (Psalm 51:10). Then David married Bathsheba, and they had a son named Solomon.

Solomon is Anointed King and Asks for Wisdom

1 Kings 1:28-40; 3:1-15

David had other sons, but he made a promise to Bathsheba, saying, "Solomon your son shall reign after me as the next king."

When David was very old, he announced that Solomon would be his heir. Zadok the priest and Nathan the prophet blew trumpets to get people to listen. They led Solomon on David's donkey to a special place and anointed him with oil as the king to sit on David's throne.

The people were happy. They rejoiced greatly and shouted, "Long live King Solomon!"

Then God came to Solomon in a dream and asked," What gift would you like me to give you?" Solomon told God that he wanted the gift of wisdom more than anything else. God was pleased with Solomon's request and gave him wisdom to tell the difference between right and wrong.

King Solomon wrote many wise sayings like those found in the book of Proverbs:

> *Trust in the LORD with all your heart,*
> *and do not rely on your own insight.*
> *In all your ways acknowledge him,*
> *and he will make straight your paths.*
> *Be not wise in your own eyes; fear the Lord,*
> *and turn away from evil.*
> *It will be healing to your flesh and*
> *refreshment to your bones.*
> *– Proverbs 3:5-8*

Solomon Builds God's Temple

1 Kings 8:1-21; 9:1-9; 11:7-13

King Solomon wanted to build a house for the LORD God. So, when the country was at peace, Solomon started building a beautiful temple in Jerusalem. He built it on Mount Moriah, where Abraham and Isaac had made a sacrifice long ago.

After the Temple was completed, the priests brought the Ark of the Covenant there. They placed it in the inner sanctuary of the Temple. Two golden angels, or **cherubim**, sat atop the Ark. Their wings were spread open as a throne for God. Just as the glory of the LORD had filled the Tabernacle in the wilderness, so did the glory of the LORD fill the Temple in Jerusalem. This became the center of worship for all of Israel.

Then God renewed the covenant he had made with Solomon's father, David. He told Solomon, "Your kingdom will last forever, but you and all the people will need to obey me and always keep my commandments." God warned them not to worship other gods. The Temple would be destroyed if they turned away from the LORD God.

King Solomon was happy with the Temple he had built for the LORD. He built more buildings and walls around many cities in Israel. Eventually, Solomon had so much money and land that he became known as not only the wisest king but also the richest.

Though Solomon was a good and wise king at first, he did not act so wisely later. He kept too much wealth for himself, and he was influenced by his many wives who worshipped false idols. He allowed his heart to turn away from God. These actions set the stage for a dark time to come.

What do you think?

1. Who do you know that is very wise?
2. Imagine what you might see if you walked into the Temple that Solomon built.
3. How do you show God you are sorry when you have made a wrong choice?

DIVIDED KINGDOM: Part I

Because the narrative jumps back and forth between the two kingdoms, Part I will look at the events of the ten tribes of the Northern Kingdom called Israel, and Part II will cover events of the two tribes in the Southern Kingdom called Judah.

“IF THIS PEOPLE GO UP TO OFFER SACRIFICES IN THE HOUSE OF THE LORD AT JERUSALEM, THEN THE HEART OF THIS PEOPLE WILL TURN AGAIN TO ... [THE] KING OF JUDAH.”

—1 Kings 12:27

Chapter Thirteen

The Kingdom of Israel Divides: Events of the Northern Kingdom of Israel

1 Kings , 2 Kings

The people of Israel did not keep God's covenant, and the kingdom divided after the death of King Solomon. The Northern Kingdom was called Israel and included ten tribes; their king was Jeroboam. The Southern Kingdom was called Judah and included the two tribes of Judah and Benjamin; Rehoboam reigned there. This chapter shares the events of the Northern Kingdom of Israel, where there were only bad kings.

Bible Reading Checklist

- [ ] 1 KINGS 11; 12; 16:23-34 The kingdom divides
- [ ] 1 KINGS 17 Miracles of Elijah the prophet
- [ ] 1 KINGS 18:17-46 Elijah Defeats the prophets of Baal and Asherah
- [ ] 2 KINGS 2:1-22 Elisha succeeds Elijah
- [ ] HOSEA 11; JOEL 2:1-14 Rebellion and prophecy of judgment

Optional: JONAH Jonah and the big fish

The Kingdom Divides

1 Kings 11; 12; 16:23-34

After King Solomon died, his son Rehoboam became king. King Rehoboam made a bad decision that caused the Kingdom of Israel to split apart. He asked his advisors, "How should I govern the people?" The older advisors warned, "Do not make the people work too hard; treat them with kindness." The younger advisors suggested just the opposite. They said, "Treat the people harshly and make them work harder than they did for King Solomon!"

Rehoboam listened to the younger advisors. The people were already burdened, but he told them that they would have to work harder than before. The people became angry. Ten of the twelve tribes of Israel refused to let him be their king. They chose a man named Jeroboam to rule them instead.

The ten tribes who followed Jeroboam broke from the other two tribes. They formed the Northern Kingdom, called Israel. King Rehoboam was left to govern only two tribes, Judah and Benjamin. These two tribes formed the Southern Kingdom, called Judah.

Jerusalem and the Temple were located in the Southern Kingdom. The people in the Northern Kingdom stopped going to Jerusalem to worship in Solomon's Temple and were cut off from knowledge of God. They set up false places of worship in the cities of Dan and Bethel. Because of this division, the two kingdoms were at war with each other for many years.

Miracles of Elijah the Prophet

1 Kings 17

Many years after the kingdom was first divided, Ahab, son of Omri, became king of the Northern Kingdom. King Ahab did many evil things. He married a woman named Jezebel who worshiped the false gods **Baal** and **Asherah**. He began to worship them too, forgetting about the true God. Jezebel and her husband, King Ahab, hated God's prophets. They especially disliked Elijah, a prophet of God who wore a hairy garment with a leather belt (see 2 Kings 1:8).

God was angry because of the altars that were set up to worship Baal and Asherah. Elijah took God's message to King Ahab, telling him, "There will be no dew nor rainfall for three years." To protect Elijah, God said to him, "Go away from here and hide near a brook. I will send ravens to bring you bread and meat."

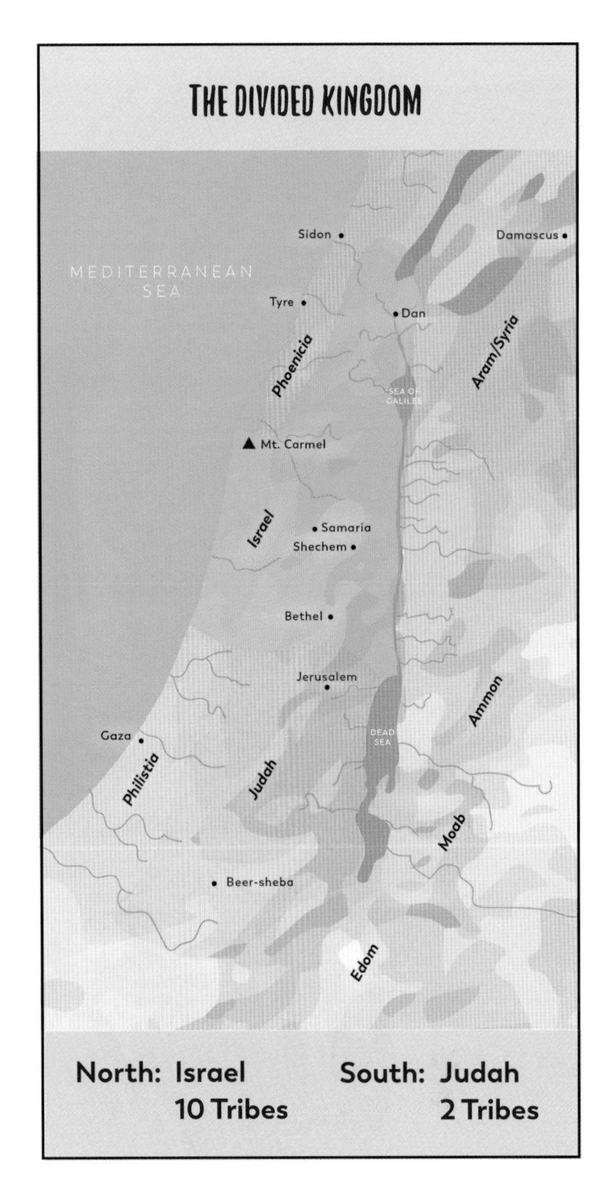

When the brook dried up because of the drought, Elijah went to a widow's house to find food and drink. She only had enough oil and flour to prepare one more meal for herself and her son. Nevertheless, she made a cake of bread and gave it to Elijah. Then God performed a miracle. He made the jar of flour and pitcher of oil last for three years, until the end of the drought! Later, when the widow's son became sick and died, God performed another miracle through Elijah. Elijah took the boy by the hand and raised him from the dead!

Elijah Defeats the Prophets of Baal and Asherah

1 Kings 18:17-46

Elijah continued to prophesy to King Ahab. "Let's have a contest to see who worships the true God," Elijah said to the king. "Bring your 450 prophets of Baal and 400 prophets of Asherah to Mount Carmel. We will each offer a sacrifice. The prophets of Baal and Asherah will sacrifice a bull to their gods. I will sacrifice a bull to the God of Israel. The sacrifice that burns will show us the god we will serve."

So they all went to Mount Carmel with two bulls for the sacrifices. Ahab and Jezebel's prophets set up an altar with the sacrifice and called on Baal and Asherah to send fire. All day long, the prophets of Baal danced, prayed, and even cut themselves with knives to get the attention of their false god, but there was no answer.

Then Elijah prepared his altar for the sacrifice. First, he poured water over it and around it so that it was drenched. Next, he called upon the LORD. God immediately sent fire from heaven that burned up the sacrificial bull. Showing his might, he also completely lapped up the water and consumed the dust.

When the people saw this, they all knelt down and shouted, "The LORD is God!" Then it began to rain, and the long drought was over.

Queen Jezebel was angry when she heard that Elijah had defeated the prophets of Baal and Asherah. Elijah was afraid she would have him killed, so he escaped to the Southern Kingdom of Judah for safety.

Elisha Succeeds Elijah

2 Kings 2:1-22

Later, God spoke to Elijah, saying," Go and find a man named Elisha, who will be your servant. Elisha will take your place as my prophet."

Elisha became Elijah's faithful helper. He learned how to be a prophet by working with Elijah for several years.

Finally, the time came for Elijah to go and be with God forever. The two prophets walked by the Jordan River. Elijah took off his cape, rolled it up, and hit the water with it. The river divided so that the two men could cross over it on dry land.

When they reached the other side, a chariot of fire suddenly swooped down and picked up Elijah. He sailed into heaven on the chariot of fire, and Elisha was left alone on the ground.

Elisha picked up the cape that Elijah had dropped, and he put it on. Then he went back to Samaria, the capital of the Northern Kingdom.

Elisha told the evil kings to repent and obey God. Elisha also helped many people as God worked miracles through him.

Sadly, the kings didn't listen to him. After Elisha died, the ten tribes of the Northern Kingdom of Israel continued to suffer under the kings' sinful rule.

Rebellion and Prophecy of Judgment

Hosea 11; Joel 2:1-14

Other prophets of God, like Hosea and Joel, warned the kings of the Northern Kingdom that they must follow the ways of God and urged the people to return to God.

Hosea reminded the people of the north of how much God loved them. He called on the people to return to God and stop worshiping idols. He also warned them that the army of the **Assyrians** would defeat the Northern Kingdom.

The prophets said that God wanted them to turn their hearts back to him so he could save them from their enemies. They reminded the people of how much God loved them, but the people continued to reject him.

Jonah and the Big Fish

Jonah

Jonah was another prophet, but he did not always obey God. In the city of Nineveh, the people worshiped false gods and treated each other very badly. God told Jonah," Go to Nineveh and tell the people to repent."

Jonah didn't want to go. Instead, he got in a boat headed in the opposite direction! When a severe storm hit, Jonah realized that it was because he was running away from God. He told the sailors to throw him overboard.

Jonah sank in the water until a giant fish swallowed him whole. He spent three days and nights in the belly of the fish. While he was there, Jonah repented and promised to obey God.

The fish threw him up onto the shore. Jonah headed straight to Nineveh to proclaim God's Word to the people there. The people listened to Jonah and were sorry for what they had done. They promised to stop doing evil things. Then God forgave them in his great mercy.

What do you think?

1. How does God want us to act toward our family and friends?
2. When people disagree, what is a good way to settle it?
3. Who can give you good advice when you are trying to make a difficult decision?

"BUT YOU SHALL FEAR THE LORD YOUR GOD,
AND HE WILL DELIVER YOU OUT
OF THE HAND OF ALL YOUR ENEMIES."

—2 Kings 17:39

Chapter Fourteen

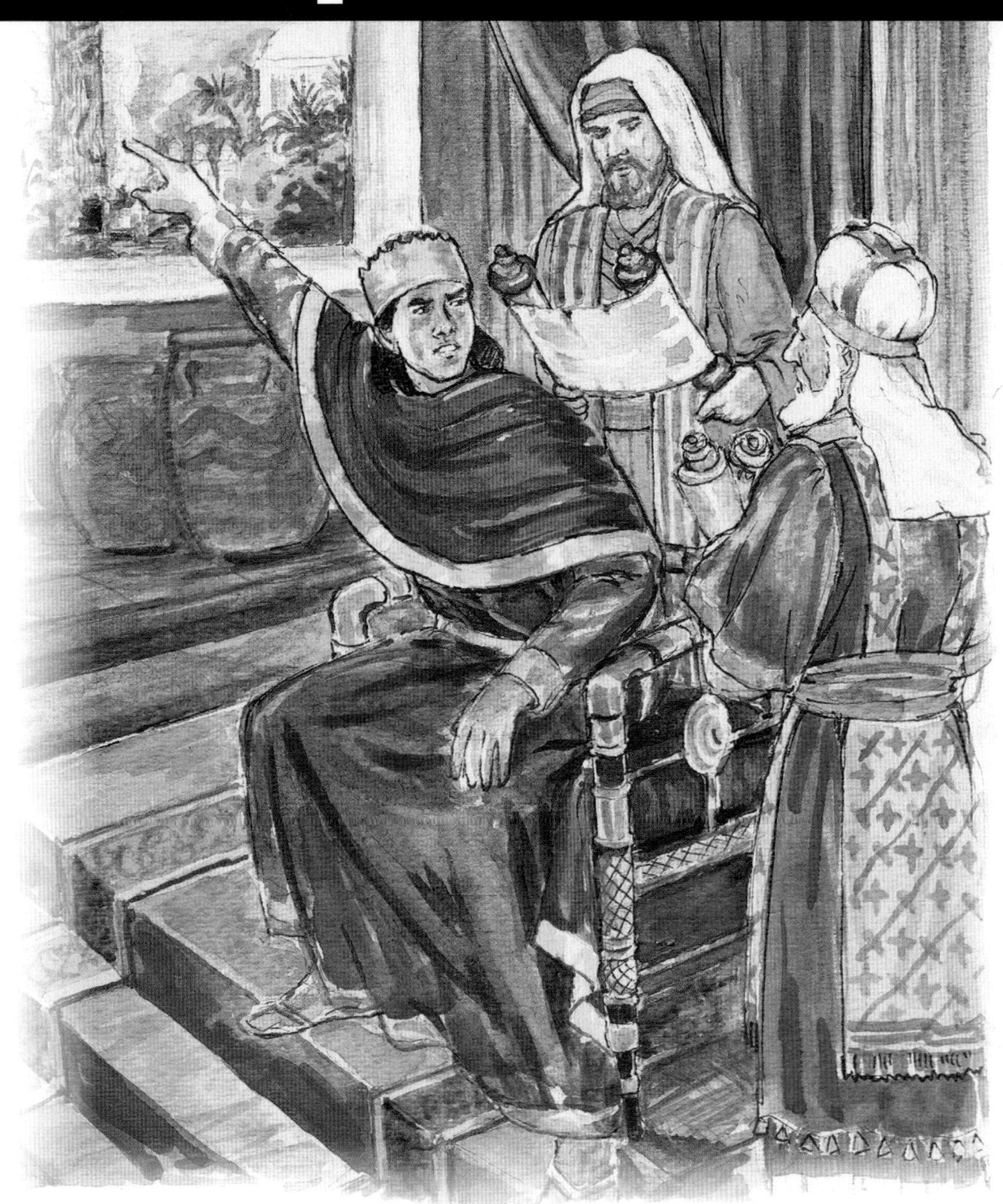

The Kingdoms of Israel and Judah Are Conquered: Events of the Southern Kingdom of Judah

1 Kings , 2 Kings

Unlike the North, which was ruled only by bad kings, the Southern Kingdom of Judah was ruled by some good kings and some bad kings. The events of the Southern Kingdom are shared in this chapter. In spite of warnings by the prophets, the Divided Kingdoms of Israel and Judah struggled for many years as the hearts of the people turned away from God.

Bible Reading Checklist

- [ ] 1 KINGS 14:21-31 King Rehoboam Reigns in the South
- [ ] 2 KINGS 11-12:3 Good King Joash
- [ ] 2 KINGS 18:1-12; 20 A sign for King Hezekiah
- [ ] 2 KINGS 21:1-6; 22; 23:1-4, 21-36 The reforms of good King Josiah
- [ ] 2 KINGS 24 The last days of the Kingdom of Judah

Optional: JEREMIAH 18:1-17; 31:1-14, 31-34 The prophet Jeremiah warns Israel and Judah

King Rehoboam Reigns in the South

1 Kings 14:21-31

After the division of the Kingdom of Israel into the North and the South, King Rehoboam, son of King Solomon, continued to rule the Southern Kingdom of Judah. He reigned for seventeen years from the capital of Jerusalem. Rehoboam was not faithful to God, and the people of Judah followed him in sinning against God. They acted like the nations around them by worshiping idols and making false sacrifices. In the fifth year of the reign of King Rehoboam, Egypt attacked Jerusalem and stole all the treasures of the Temple.

There was constant war between the Southern and Northern Kingdoms while Rehoboam reigned in the south and Jeroboam reigned in the north.

Over time, the Southern Kingdom of Judah and the Northern Kingdom of Israel were ruled by many different kings. Each of the kings of the Northern Kingdom turned away from God. They worshiped idols and did not care for the poor. Many of the kings of the Southern Kingdom did the same, but not all. The kingdoms continued to fight each other, and both kingdoms fought with outside nations as well.

Good King Joash

2 Kings 11–12:3

Later, a bad queen named Athaliah ruled the Southern Kingdom of Judah. Because of her jealousy, she ordered the killing of the entire royal family.

One baby boy named Joash was hidden away and spared. He was protected by the priests in the Temple. When he was seven years old, the priest Jehoiada declared him as the king. "Long live the king!" the people shouted.

Queen Athaliah was enraged! She wanted to be the only ruler, but she was killed, and King Joash (also called Jehoash) became the king of Judah.

Joash was a good king. He listened to Jehoiada the priest, who knew the laws of God. Joash obeyed God and told the priests to repair the house of the LORD with money donated to the Temple. He reigned for forty years in Jerusalem.

A Sign for King Hezekiah

2 Kings 18:1-12; 20

Some years after the reign of King Joash in the Southern Kingdom, there was another good king, whose name was Hezekiah.

Hezekiah was the son of a wicked king, Ahaz. Unlike his father, King Hezekiah restored the altars to the LORD God. He encouraged the people to obey God's laws. Hezekiah trusted God, and the LORD was with him wherever he went.

While Hezekiah was king in the south, the Northern Kingdom of Israel was conquered by an army from **Assyria**. King Hezekiah knew that the same thing could happen to the Southern Kingdom of Judah if the people turned away from God. He told his priests to offer sacrifices only to the LORD God. He prayed to God every day for strength and courage to be a good king.

Once, when Hezekiah was sick, he prayed to God for healing. The prophet Isaiah came to him and told him, "God says you will not die."

King Hezekiah said, "Please give me a sign that this prophecy will come true."

Isaiah told him the sun would go backward ten steps on the sundial. It would be as if time went in reverse. Miraculously, that is what happened! Three days later, King Hezekiah was well again. He lived another fifteen years to rule the Kingdom of Judah.

The Reforms of Good King Josiah

2 Kings 21:1-6; 22; 23:1-4, 21-36

King Hezekiah's son Manasseh was a wicked king. He set up an idol in the Temple and led the people away from God. He was so evil that he burned his own son as a sacrifice to a false god.

Most of the kings who reigned in the Kingdom of Judah after Manasseh also did evil things. However, there was another good king, named Josiah. He was eight years old when he became king. King Josiah loved the LORD, and he helped the people turn away from idol worship.

Josiah asked the priests to repair and clean the Temple. During the cleaning, the high priest, Hilkiah, found the **Book of the Law of Moses**. He gave the book to Josiah to read.

When Josiah read the words of God, he was sorry for not obeying God, and he made a covenant to keep the LORD's commandments. He tore down the Asherah pole that King Manasseh had put in the Temple for idol worship. He destroyed all the altars to false gods throughout the land. He also commanded that the Feast of Passover be celebrated again. It had been many years since that holy festival had been observed.

Unfortunately, this was the last time that a good king reigned in Judah.

During fighting between the **Assyrians** and **Babylonians**, Pharaoh Neco came up from Egypt to join the Assyrians. When he passed through the Southern Kingdom, King Josiah went out to fight him in the valley of **Megiddo**. King Josiah was killed there, and his son was exiled to Egypt.

The Last Days of the Kingdom of Judah

2 Kings 24

The pharaoh appointed another son of Josiah as king of Judah, who then taxed his people and gave the money to the pharaoh. The Babylonians became very strong. Eventually, their king, Nebuchadnezzar, came to Jerusalem. He took all the treasures from the Temple and captured the royal family and the leaders of Jerusalem.

> *Behold, the days are coming, says the Lord, when I will make a new covenant with the house of Israel and the house of Judah ... But this is the covenant which I will make with the house of Israel after those days, says the Lord: I will put my law within them, and I will write it upon their heart; and I will be their God, and they shall be my people.*
>
> – Jeremiah 31:31, 33

The Prophet Jeremiah Warns Israel and Judah

Jeremiah 18:1-17; 31:1-14, 31-34

Jeremiah was a great prophet during this time. He prophesied to both the Kingdoms of Israel and Judah. God spoke through him to tell people that they were suffering because they would not obey his laws. Jeremiah said that God is like a potter who molds his people like clay into the good and wonderful people he created them to be. He would do this if they would obey him. Jeremiah prophesied about a coming day when God would make a new covenant with Israel and Judah. In that future time, their love for God would come from the heart.

What do you think?

1. What are the things in life that might lead us away from God?
2. What happens to a group when their leader chooses to do good things?
3. How do you stay mindful of the Ten Commandments in your life?

EXILE

BY THE WATERS OF BABYLON, THERE WE SAT DOWN AND WEPT, WHEN WE REMEMBERED ZION.

—Psalm 137:1

Chapter Fifteen

The Exiles Mourn Over Jerusalem

2 Kings, Daniel

After years of failing to listen to the prophets and struggling to obey God, both the Northern and Southern Kingdoms were conquered by foreign nations. The Northern Kingdom of Israel was conquered by the Assyrians in 722 BC. The Southern Kingdom of Judah fell to Babylon in 587 BC. The people from the Northern Kingdom were mixed into other cultures. The people from the Southern Kingdom of Judah were known as Jews from this time forward. Many of the people were taken away from their homes and forced into exile in foreign lands. God works through his prophets Jeremiah and Daniel to remind his people that he has not forgotten them.

Bible Reading Checklist

- [ ] **2 KINGS 17** Assyria conquers the Northern Kingdom; foreign possession of Samaria
- [ ] **2 KINGS 25:1-21; JEREMIAH 38:1-6; PSALM 137:1-4** Babylon conquers the Southern Kingdom; the exiles weep
- [ ] **DANIEL 2** Daniel interprets the king's vision
- [ ] **DANIEL 3** Three men in the fiery furnace
- [ ] **DANIEL 6** Daniel and the lions' den

Assyria Conquers the Northern Kingdom

2 Kings 17:1-23

The King of Assyria invaded the Northern Kingdom of Israel. The Assyrians robbed and looted the Israelites' homes, stealing the things they used for idol worship.

The capital of the Northern Kingdom, Samaria, was built on a hill, so it was hard to capture. The Assyrians surrounded Samaria and would not let the people get food or water. The Israelites were starving and dying, so they eventually gave up their city.

The Assyrians killed King Hoshea and carried the people away as slaves. The ten tribes of the Northern Kingdom of Israel were lost among the foreign nations, and they never returned to the Promised Land.

THE KINGDOMS OF ISRAEL AND JUDAH ARE CONQUERED

722 BC	The Northern Kingdom of Israel falls to Assyria.
587 BC	The Southern Kingdom of Judah falls to Babylon and remains in exile for seventy years.

Foreign Possession of Samaria

2 Kings 17:24-41

Then the king of Assyria brought his own people from five foreign lands to settle around the city of Samaria, where the Israelites used to live. The foreigners settled into the Israelites' homes and worshiped their false gods.

When lions came into their towns and attacked them, they were afraid. They told the king of Assyria that the God of Israel had sent the lions to kill them because they did not know how to worship him. So the king of Assyria sent some of the exiled priests back to Samaria to teach the people their religious customs, including the first commandment, which says, "You shall have no other gods before me" (Exodus 20:3).

The people did not really learn how to worship the God of Israel. Instead, they just copied what the priests did but continued to worship their own false gods at the same time. They did not follow the commandments God gave to his people through Moses. This group of people came to be known as the **Samaritans**.

Babylon Conquers the Southern Kingdom

2 Kings 25:1-21; Jeremiah 38:1-6

The Southern Kingdom was weak. They had been constantly fighting with the tribes in the Northern Kingdom. They were also spiritually weak because they had disobeyed God so many times.

The prophet Jeremiah warned the people that they would be conquered because of their refusal to turn away from their false gods. The people became angry at this prophecy. They threw Jeremiah into a muddy *cistern,* or well. Finally, King Nebuchadnezzar of **Babylon** attacked Judah. He took the people into captivity just as it had happened to the Northern Kingdom many years earlier. The people were carried away with their hands and feet tied. The king's sons were killed, and King Zedekiah was blinded and thrown into prison in Babylon.

After that, King Nebuchadnezzar's men went to the Temple in Jerusalem. They broke into pieces the bronze pillars that King Solomon had made for the house of the Lord. They took the bronze back to Babylon along with all the pots, shovels, and snuffers, the dishes for incense, and all the other sacred vessels used in the Temple. Then they burned down the houses, including the house of the Lord, so that they were completely destroyed. Lastly, they captured the priests that served in the Temple and carried them back to Babylon, where they killed them.

The Exiles Weep

Psalm 137

This sad part of the story is called the Exile because God's people were taken away from the Promised Land and forced to live in a foreign place. Only a small group of the Israelite people stayed behind to take care of the vineyards and olive trees.

The exiles in Babylon wept for **Zion,** the hill in Jerusalem where the Temple had stood. In their homesickness, the name *Zion* came to represent the entire city of Jerusalem, their home and God's home, the spiritual center of the people of Israel. Their sin had led not only to their separation from their land but to a separation from God.

Daniel Interprets the King's Vision

Daniel 2

The people from the Kingdom of Judah became known as the Jewish people. While they were in exile in Babylon, many of the Jewish people still loved God and wanted to worship him properly. One of these faithful people was a young man named Daniel.

Daniel was smart and strong, and God had prepared him to be a prophet. King Nebuchadnezzar of Babylon saw how smart Daniel was and took him to work in his royal palace.

One night, Nebuchadnezzar had a strange dream. His advisors didn't know how to interpret it. The dream was about a huge statue. The head was made of gold, the chest and arms were silver, and the stomach and thighs were bronze. The statue's legs were iron, and its feet were made partly of iron and partly of clay. Someone, not a person, cut out a stone and broke the statue's feet with it. Then the whole statue broke apart.

Daniel offered to pray to God to find out what the dream meant. He prayed, "Blessed be God forever! He has shown me what the dream means."

Daniel told the king God's meaning. King Nebuchadnezzar's statue represented five kingdoms. The gold head was the Babylonian kingdom. After Babylon, **Persia** would rule, represented by the

silver chest and arms. Then Greece, another kingdom, would rise, represented by the bronze belly and thighs. After that, Rome, symbolized by the legs of iron. The fifth kingdom, represented by the stone, was the one that God himself would set up. That kingdom would bring an end to all the other kingdoms and would last forever.

We understand now that the last kingdom is the kingdom of God (see CCC 2816-2820).

King Nebuchadnezzar was impressed by Daniel's interpretation of his dream. He made Daniel the ruler over the province of Babylon.

Three Men in the Fiery Furnace

Daniel 3

King Nebuchadnezzar was still attached to false gods. He made a large image of gold and commanded all of the people to bow down and worship it.

Three Jews in exile, named Shadrach, Meshach, and Abednego, refused to bow down before the king's idol. The angry king shouted, "If you do not bow down to my idol, you will be thrown into the fiery furnace!"

They answered, "We will not serve your false gods! Our God is able to save us!"

The king was furious and ordered them to be thrown into a furnace. While the three men were in the fire, an angel of the LORD came to be with them. The angel protected them from harm. The men blessed God and sang his praises while the flames burned around them.

King Nebuchadnezzar was amazed at this miracle, and he proclaimed, "The God of Shadrach, Meshach, and Abednego has delivered them. Blessed be God!" Then the king decreed that no one should ever again say anything against their God.

Daniel and the Lions' Den

Daniel 6

After Nebuchadnezzar, King Darius ruled in Babylon. Daniel still had great responsibility in the court. Some officers were jealous of him and plotted against him. They said, "Let's make the king sign a law that no one can worship anyone but the king."

When they found Daniel worshiping God instead, they brought him to King Darius. They told the king, "Daniel has broken the new law and must be thrown into a den of lions!"

King Darius liked Daniel, but he could not break his own law. He ordered that Daniel be cast into the den with the lions.

God sent his angel to be with Daniel and saved him from death by closing the mouths of the lions. The king was astonished at God's saving power. He decreed, "The God of Daniel is the living God! Everyone in Babylon shall honor him!"

The Jewish people were in exile in Babylon for seventy years. During their captivity, they remembered all the wonderful things God had done in the past. They had a change of heart. They began to understand that God's judgment is always right and his mercy is endless. They looked forward to the day when they would be able to return home to Jerusalem.

Look on my affliction and deliver me, for I do not forget thy law.
Plead my cause and redeem me; give me life according to thy promise!
Salvation is far from the wicked, for they do not seek thy statutes.
Great is thy mercy, O Lord; give me life according to thy justice.

– Psalm 119:153-156

What do you think?

1. Describe how good things can sometimes come from a bad experience.
2. How do you find the courage to do the right thing?
3. Do you ever feel far away from God? How do you become closer to him?

RETURN

FOR HE IS GOOD, FOR HIS STEADFAST LOVE ENDURES FOR EVER TOWARD ISRAEL.

—Ezra 3:11

Chapter Sixteen

The Exiles Return to Jerusalem

Ezra, Nehemiah

After years of exile in Babylon, the Jewish people of the former Kingdom of Judah begin to return to their homes in Jerusalem. They return in three groups, led by Zerubbabel, Ezra, and Nehemiah. They begin the work of rebuilding the Temple and the walls around the city of Jerusalem. They also begin to relearn the laws that were given to Moses. Some of the Jewish people remained in the land of Babylon, which became Persia, where Queen Esther saved her people from death.

Bible Reading Checklist

- ☐ EZRA 1–2:2 King Cyrus allows the exiles to return
- ☐ EZRA 3–4:4 The foundations of the Temple are laid
- ☐ EZRA 7:1-10; 9-10:5 Ezra returns to Jerusalem
- ☐ NEHEMIAH 1-2:20; 4 The wall around Jerusalem is rebuilt
- ☐ NEHEMIAH 8 Ezra reads the Book of the Law of Moses

Optional: ESTHER 1-9 Esther saves her people

King Cyrus Allows the Exiles to Return

Ezra 1–2:2

The Kingdom of Babylon soon lost its influence. Persia, led by King Cyrus, became more powerful, and the land that was once called Babylon was now called Persia. Many exiles from the Kingdom of Judah still lived as slaves there.

In Jerusalem, the Temple that Solomon had built for God had been destroyed by the Babylonians. King Cyrus told the exiles, "Return to Jerusalem! Rebuild your Temple and bring offerings to give to your God!"

One of the exiles, Zerubbabel, was appointed governor of Judah. He and Jeshua, the priest, led the exiles back.

It was a very exciting time! They brought back the sacred cups and washbasins, gold and silver, and animals to sacrifice to the LORD. The people returned to the towns where their families had lived before their capture. Then they gathered in Jerusalem and built an altar so they could start making offerings to the LORD.

They sang, "God is good, and his mercy endures forever!" They celebrated the **Feast of Booths** and joyfully worshiped the God of their ancestors.

The Foundations of the Temple Are Laid

Ezra 3–4:4

Next, Zerubbabel and Jeshua hired masons and carpenters. They bought building materials to repair the Temple. They brought cedar trees from **Lebanon** to use for lumber. They appointed priests from the tribe of the Levites to oversee the work.

When the builders finally lay the foundation stone in place, they had a big celebration. The priests came dressed in their holy vestments and played trumpets. Other Levites followed behind playing loud cymbals, praising the LORD with their music.

People came from all around to celebrate. Some were very happy and shouted with tears of joy, and others were sad because they remembered the beauty of the previous Temple built by King Solomon. Their shouts of joy and cries of sadness mingled together and were heard by people all around.

When some of their neighbors saw that Jerusalem was being rebuilt, they were jealous. They complained to the new king of Persia, Artaxerxes, and he ordered the Jews to stop work. They had to wait until a new king came into power before they could finish rebuilding the Temple.

Ezra Returns to Jerusalem

Ezra 7:1-10, 9-10:5

After some time, a new king replaced Artaxerxes in Persia. His name was Darius. King Darius gave the **Jews** permission to start rebuilding the Temple again. He gave them building materials and supplies to make sacrifices to God—a pretty amazing thing for a foreign king to do.

Ezra the scribe led a group of exiles to Jerusalem to continue the work. Once again, they celebrated as they dedicated their work to God with joy. In the following months and years, they remembered to celebrate all the important holidays, like the **Feast of Passover** and the **Feast of Unleavened Bread**.

Unfortunately, the people forgot one very important commandment: They forgot that they were not supposed to worship false gods. They married people from the surrounding nations and began to worship the gods of those other nations. This was a serious problem, and many people were hurt because of the bad example set by the leaders and priests.

Ezra was a priest from the line of Aaron, who helped the people remember the Law of Moses. Ezra prayed, "O Lord God, I am ashamed that we have sinned against you. Please have mercy on us."

As Ezra was praying, people began to cry as they realized what they had done. They were very sorry and decided to make things right again. They turned away from the false gods of the other nations and sent the wives and children back to their own families. Then they took an oath, saying, "We will be faithful to God once again!"

The Wall Around Jerusalem Is Rebuilt

Nehemiah 1-2:20; 4

Many more exiles returned to Jerusalem with the prophet Nehemiah. Nehemiah had heard that the wall of Jerusalem was broken down and the gates destroyed. The wall was very important because it went around the entire city to keep the people safe inside. Nehemiah was eager to rebuild it.

Many enemies of Jerusalem had tried to get the people to stop building the wall, but Nehemiah was brave. He trusted in the LORD to help them. Finally, they finished the wall, and the city was protected. Parts of this wall are still visible in the city of Jerusalem today.

Ezra Reads the Book of the Law of Moses

Nehemiah 8

When the wall of Jerusalem had been rebuilt, the people gathered inside the city near the Water Gate to hear something very important. Ezra the priest brought out the Book of the Law of Moses that the LORD had given the Israelites.

Ezra began to read the book aloud to everyone: men, women, and children who were old enough to understand the words. Everyone listened carefully and happily as Ezra read God's Word to them. When he finished, the priests helped him explain what the reading meant, and the people understood.

Ezra said, "This day is holy, so be happy! *The joy of the Lord is your strength!*" Then everyone celebrated with shouts of thanksgiving, singing, and playing musical instruments!

Their long exile was over. People were once again free to worship in Jerusalem at the newly rebuilt Temple. They could read and study the words of the Law of Moses whenever they wanted to. All of these things helped them have a better relationship with God and with one another.

God had restored the Jews by bringing them back to Jerusalem to rebuild the Temple and the wall around the city. Their joy was renewed while they heard the life-giving words from the Book of the Law of Moses. We call this period the Return. God had promised many times through his prophets that he would restore his people. He is always ready to bless his people and lead them back into the safety of his kingdom.

Esther Saves Her People

Esther: 1-9

While many of the Jewish people returned to the land of Israel, some were still in Persia. One of them was a faithful young woman named Esther.

Esther, her cousin Mordecai, and their family lived in the city of Susa, the capital

of Persia. The king of Persia at that time was named Ahasuerus (also known as Artaxerxes). When Ahasuerus needed a wife, he chose Esther, and she became the queen of Persia.

Ahasuerus was kind to the Jewish people living in Persia, but his servant Haman was not. Haman plotted to kill the Jewish people. When Esther learned about Haman's plot, she was afraid. She asked her cousin Mordecai what to do.

Mordecai said, *"You might have been placed in the kingdom for such a time as this."* Esther prayed for courage. Then she bravely told King Ahasuerus about Haman's plot.

The King loved Esther and her cousin Mordecai, so he put a stop to the evil plans Haman had made. Then he appointed Mordecai as his servant instead of Haman. And from that day forth, all the Jews remember the time with a holiday called **Purim**, when they celebrate Esther's bravery in saving the Jewish people from death.

What do you think?

1. What can happen if we only keep the laws of God that we find easy and don't keep the ones that seem hard?
2. Why do we hear the Bible read aloud at every Mass?
3. Is there a place where you experience God's presence with joy?

WE WILL NOT OBEY THE KING'S WORDS BY TURNING ASIDE FROM OUR RELIGION TO THE RIGHT HAND OR TO THE LEFT.

—1 Maccabees 2:22

Chapter Seventeen

The Maccabees Defend the Faith

1 Maccabees

After many of the Jews returned to Jerusalem from Persia, Greece became a new world power. The Greeks tried to impose the Greek language, culture, and religion on the whole world. The Jews refused to worship foreign gods and were punished. In spite of being persecuted, a Jewish priest named Mattathias and his son, Judas Maccabeus, fought to keep the laws of God. This is known as the Maccabean Revolt.

Bible Reading Checklist

- [ ] 1 MACCABEES 1:1-19 The Greek Empire comes to power
- [ ] 1 MACCABEES 1:20-63 Greek persecution of the Jews
- [ ] Optional: 2 MACCABEES 7 The woman and her martyred sons
- [ ] 1 MACCABEES 2–3:2 Mattathias and his sons revolt
- [ ] 1 MACCABEES 4:36-59 Purification of the Temple
- [ ] 2 MACCABEES 12:39-45 Prayers for the dead

The Greek Empire Comes to Power

1 Maccabees 1:1-19

Over time, Greece became the strongest power in the world. The Greek empire grew under the military leadership of Alexander the Great. He conquered Persia and then most of the known world.

Alexander the Great died in his early thirties, and his empire was divided among his three generals. Greek was the main language spoken during this time. Even the Hebrew Scriptures were translated into Greek.

Hellenism is a word that describes Greek world culture. The whole world was "hellenized" by Greek customs, language, and religion. For the Jews, these customs often conflicted with the laws God had given to his people. The Greeks worshiped many **mythological,** or false, gods such as Zeus and Hercules.

Greek Persecution of the Jews

1 Maccabees 1:20-63

The Seleucids were the Greek people who became the governors of the Promised Land. A Seleucid ruler named Antiochus Epiphanes ruled over the southern region, now called **Judea,** and Jerusalem. He entered the Jewish Temple and took the sacred vessels away.

Antiochus was cruel, and he persecuted the Jews. He made a decree to force all the inhabitants of Judea to worship the way the Greeks did. The Greek law required them to bow down to idols and offer sacrifices that were forbidden by God.

Antiochus sent people to Judea to offer unholy sacrifices on God's altar. Antiochus would not allow the Jews to circumcise their boys, which is the Jewish sign of their covenant with God. The Greeks burned the books of God's Law. Anyone who would not obey the new decree was put to death.

The Woman and Her Martyred Sons

2 Maccabees 7

During this time of Greek oppression, many Jews continued to follow the Law of God. They refused to obey the laws of the Greeks.

One of these heroic Jewish people was a brave mother with seven sons. She had raised her sons to be faithful to the God of Israel. Antiochus told the mother and her sons that they had to bow to a Greek statue and eat pork. Eating pork was forbidden under Jewish law.

The evil king said he would kill the family if they refused. The mother and her sons chose to obey God and refused to bow down to the Greek statue or eat pork. They chose to die rather than disobey God. One by one, the sons were killed in front of their mother. She gave them

courage, saying, "God in his mercy will give life back to you after this life has ended!" All of them remained brave.

Finally, after all her sons were cruelly killed, the mother was also killed. They all believed that they would see God after they died, so they chose to die rather than disobey God (see CCC 633-637). People who die for their faith are called **martyrs**.

Mattathias and His Sons Revolt

1 Maccabees 2–3:2

In the town of Modein in Judea, there was a devout priest named Mattathias who had five sons. Antiochus sent his officials there to offer silver and gold to people if they would make sacrifices of unclean animals to pagan gods. This was forbidden by Jewish Law.

Mattathias would not do it, and he would not allow anyone else to do it either. He said, *"Let everyone who is zealous for the law and supports the covenant come out with me!"* This was the start of the Maccabean Revolt.

Mattathias killed the government official and chased the others away. Then he and his sons hid in the wilderness, for they would be arrested if caught. Many Jews joined them to fight the Seleucids.

After many years of battle, Mattathias died, and his son Judas became the leader. Judas Maccabeus was a hero. He fought bravely for the Jewish people. Finally, the rebels won back the city of Jerusalem and once again gained control of the Temple.

Purification of the Temple

1 Maccabees 4:36-59

The Temple was overgrown with bushes, and many parts were ruined. The altar had been profaned by the Greeks. They had not respected it as a holy place.

Judas Maccabeus made sure that the altar was cleaned and ritually purified by the priests. They made new holy vessels. They brought back the lampstand and the table that belonged in the Temple.

Everyone was so happy! They celebrated for eight days around the Temple, singing and dancing in the streets. Judas declared that this should be celebrated every year. Today this Jewish holiday is called **Hanukkah**.

Prayers for the Dead

2 Maccabees 12:39-45

After Antiochus Epiphanes died, his son, named Antiochus Eupator, came to power. Eupator was kinder to the Jews than his father had been. He said that they should be allowed to live as they pleased.

Sadly, some of the local governors continued to treat the Jews badly. Judas Maccabeus and his soldiers called upon God for help. They marched against those who killed the Jews.

At the end of one attack, Judas and his men went to bury their fellow soldiers who had fallen. They discovered that those who had died were wearing tokens of idols and false gods under their clothing. This is forbidden by the first commandment, which states that we must love our God and must not worship any other gods. Judas was sad that these soldiers had not trusted the LORD God. He knew they would rise from the dead someday, so he prayed that their sins would be forgiven (see CCC 1030-1032).

The Maccabean revolt lasted about seven years. It shows us how people who were devoted to God were able to fight against the culture that threatened them. The Jews knew what God wanted them to do because they prayed, obeyed God's commandments, and read the Book of the Law. God gave them courage to stand up for their faith.

In our lives today, we must be sure that we do not follow the culture when it leads us away from God. We can also know how God wants us to live by praying, obeying, and studying the Bible and *Catechism*. The same God who gave the Jews courage to stand up for what is right also gives us the courage to do what is right.

This is the last narrative book of the Old Testament. Sadly, the Maccabean dynasty, or **Maccabees** (who were also known as the **Hasmoneans**), was conquered by Rome. Judea was ruled by King Herod the Great, while Caesar Augustus was the Roman emperor. Herod fought against the Hasmoneans and took over their outposts. King Herod built many fortresses for himself. He beautified the Temple in Jerusalem not long before Jesus would be born. The stage was set for the King of Kings to come into the world.

What do you think?

1. Why do we pray for those who have died?
2. What are some things in the sanctuary of a church that remind us that it is a holy place?
3. How does God help you do the right thing when others around you are making poor choices?

AND BEHOLD, YOU WILL CONCEIVE IN YOUR WOMB AND BEAR A SON, AND YOU SHALL CALL HIS NAME JESUS.

—Luke 1:31

Chapter Eighteen

Jesus, Son of God, Is Born of Mary

Luke

As promised by God, the Messiah arrived! After the sin of Adam and Eve in the book of Genesis, God showed his great mercy when he promised salvation for all people: He would send a lamb to take away our sins. A Son of David would establish an everlasting kingdom. A worldwide blessing would come from Israel. Jesus' name means "Yahweh (God) saves." He is the Messiah, the anointed one who will bring us back to God.

Bible Reading Checklist

- [ ] **LUKE 1–2** The Birth of John the Baptist; the Birth of Jesus; the Shepherds, Simeon, and Anna Recognize the Messiah; finding the Child Jesus in the Temple
- [ ] **LUKE 3:1-22; 4:1-13** Baptism of Jesus; temptation of Jesus
- [ ] **LUKE 5:1-29; 6:12-14; JOHN 2:1-11** Jesus calls his disciples; Jesus' first miracle
- [ ] **MATTHEW 5:1-12; 8:5-13** Jesus teaches the Beatitudes; Jesus heals the centurion's servant
- [ ] **LUKE 9:1-36** Jesus gives his authority to the Twelve; Jesus feeds the five thousand; the Transfiguration

The Birth of John the Baptist

Luke 1:1-25, 57-80

A priest named Zechariah and his wife, Elizabeth, were both very old and had no children. While Zechariah was in the Temple in Jerusalem, the angel Gabriel appeared to him. Gabriel told him," You will have a son and name him John. This child will grow up to help people *prepare the way of the Lord*" (Isaiah 40:3).

Zechariah did not believe the words of the angel right away, and he became unable to speak. When the baby was born, Zechariah wrote on a tablet that the baby's name should be John. Suddenly Zechariah could speak again. He said, *"Blessed be the Lord God of Israel!"* The child grew up to become John the Baptist. He lived in the wilderness of Judea.

WILDERNESS COMMUNITIES

At the time of John the Baptist, there were several groups who wanted to live a life close to God. They lived together in communities in the wilderness, like monks who live in **monasteries** today. Some of those groups wrote texts that are part of the **Dead Sea Scrolls.**

The Birth of Jesus

Luke 1:26-56; 2:1-7

Before the birth of John the Baptist, the angel Gabriel appeared to a young girl named Mary. Gabriel said to Mary, *"Hail, O favored one, the Lord is with you."* He told her that she would have a baby who would be the Son of God. She should name him Jesus, which means "God saves."

Mary wondered how this could happen, but she trusted God and said yes.

Mary went to visit her relative Elizabeth to share the wonderful news. When Mary arrived, the baby in Elizabeth's womb jumped with joy! Elizabeth cried, *"Blessed are you among women, and blessed is the fruit of your womb!"*

Mary stayed with Elizabeth for three months. Then she returned home to her husband, Joseph, in Nazareth.

The Roman emperor, Caesar Augustus, announced a **census** of all the people in the Roman Empire. Mary and Joseph traveled to Bethlehem to be counted because that was Joseph's hometown.

While they were in Bethlehem, Jesus was born. Mary and Joseph wrapped him in **swaddling clothes** and laid him in a **manger**.

The child would also be known as **Emmanuel**, which means *"God with us"* (see Isaiah 7:14; Matthew 1:23). By taking human form, Jesus became God **incarnate**. Jesus is truly God and truly man.

"For us men and for our salvation he came down from heaven, and by the Holy Spirit was incarnate of the virgin Mary, and became man."

The Shepherds, Simeon, and Anna Recognize the Messiah

Read Luke 2:8-40

On the night Jesus was born, angels appeared to shepherds in a nearby field, praising God and saying, ***"Glory to God in the highest, and on earth peace to people of good will."*** The angels told the shepherds that a Savior had been born that very night. The shepherds hurried to visit Mary and Joseph and greet the newborn king.

THE ROSARY

Fourth Joyful Mystery

THE PRESENTATION OF JESUS

(Luke 2:22-23)

Forty days later, Mary and Joseph brought the baby Jesus to Jerusalem to be presented in the Temple in fulfillment of Jewish law.

In the Temple, two prophets recognized the baby Jesus as the Messiah. An old man named Simeon had been waiting a long time to see the Messiah. When Mary and Joseph approached Simeon, he took Jesus in his arms and said, "Now I see God's salvation!" He said that Jesus would be great, and cautioned Mary that Jesus' greatness would cause her much sorrow.

Then a prophetess named Anna came forward. She gave thanks for the baby and proclaimed that deliverance had finally come to God's people.

While Jesus was still a baby, **Magi**, who were wise men from the East, saw a new star in the sky. They believed it meant that a new king had been born (see Matthew 2:1-12).

The Magi followed the star, which led them to the baby Jesus. The Magi bowed down before him and gave him gifts of gold, frankincense, and myrrh.

Finding the Child Jesus in the Temple

Luke 2:41-52

The last story about Jesus as a young boy happened when he was twelve years old. Jesus and his family traveled with others to Jerusalem as they did every year for the Feast of the Passover. After the Passover celebration, they headed home to Nazareth. On the way, Mary and Joseph discovered that Jesus was not among the travelers. Worried, they hurried back to Jerusalem and searched many places for him.

At last they found Jesus in the Temple. He was listening to the elders and asking questions. The elders were amazed by Jesus' understanding and his wise answers.

Mary and Joseph asked, "Son, why have you done this? We have been looking for you everywhere." Jesus replied, *"Didn't you know that I must be in my Father's house?"*

Jesus returned with his parents to Nazareth and was obedient to them. There he grew from a boy to a man. He learned how to be a carpenter from his earthly father, Joseph. He also continued to study the Law of Moses, growing in wisdom until he was ready to start his ministry at about the age of thirty.

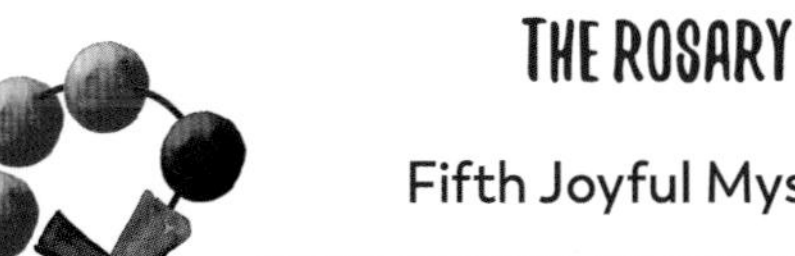

THE ROSARY

Fifth Joyful Mystery

THE FINDING OF THE CHILD JESUS IN THE TEMPLE

(Luke 2:48)

Baptism of Jesus

Luke 3:1-22

When he was grown, Elizabeth and Zechariah's son, John, began to preach about the repentance of sins. He lived in the desert and dressed in a camel-hair garment like the prophet Elijah.

John began baptizing in the Jordan River. People came from all around to be baptized for the forgiveness of their sins. They asked John if he was the Christ, but he said no. John said, *"I baptize with water, but he will baptize with the Holy Spirit and with fire. I am not even worthy to untie his sandals."*

Jesus came to be baptized even though Jesus never sinned. When Jesus received **baptism** from John, he allowed himself to be numbered among sinners. As John baptized him, a dove descended on Jesus and a voice from heaven said, *"Thou art my beloved son."*

Temptation of Jesus

Luke 4:1-13

Right after his baptism, Jesus went into the wilderness. He spent forty days there fasting and praying. Since he didn't eat anything, he was very hungry.

The devil came and tried to tempt him with food, power, and riches. With each temptation, Jesus responded to the devil by repeating words from the Bible. The devil told him to turn a stone into bread, but Jesus reminded him that we do not live by bread alone. Then the devil told him he would give him all the kingdoms of the world if he would worship him, but Jesus reminded him that we are to worship God alone. Finally, the devil told him to throw himself down from a high place and let God's angels protect him, but Jesus reminded him that we are not to tempt God.

Jesus did not give in to the temptations, so the devil left him alone. Then the angels came to take care of him.

Jesus Calls His Disciples

Luke 5:1-29; 6:12-14

Jesus came to the town of Capernaum on the shores of the Sea of Galilee. He chose twelve men to follow him. These men were the first **disciples** of Jesus. Some of these men were fishermen. He told them that one day they would be catching people instead of fish!

The men he chose were Simon, whom Jesus named Peter, and Peter's brother Andrew; James and John, the sons of Zebedee; Philip, Bartholomew, and Matthew, the tax collector; Thomas; James, son of Alphaeus; Thaddaeus; and Simon the Cananaean. Jesus also called Judas Iscariot, who later became a traitor (Luke 6:14-16). All of these men, even Judas Iscariot, were important to Jesus. He chose these men to spread the Good News to everyone.

THE TWELVE DISCIPLES (later known as apostles)

Peter	John	Matthew	Thaddaeus
Andrew	Philip	Thomas	Simon
James	Bartholomew	James	Judas Iscariot

Jesus' First Miracle

John 2:1-11

Not far from Capernaum was the small village of Cana. Jesus and Mary, his mother, were invited to a wedding there.

Toward the end of the wedding celebration, the host ran out of wine. He had nothing left to give his guests.

Mary urged Jesus to do something to help. She said to the servants, *"Do whatever he tells you."*

Jesus told the servants to fill some large jars with water. Then Jesus said, "Now draw some out and take it to the steward." They did what he asked, and when the steward tasted the water, he was amazed. It had turned into the finest wine!

Jesus Teaches the Beatitudes

Matthew 5:1-12

Jesus went to a nearby hill to preach. His disciples were with him, and people came from all around to hear him. He told them about the kingdom of God and how to be truly happy.

Jesus said, *"Blessed are the poor in spirit, for theirs is the kingdom of heaven."* He went on to say that people are happy, or blessed, when they are meek, mourning, and hungering for justice. He said people are blessed when they are merciful, pure of heart, and make peace with each other. He also said that people who suffer **persecution** and cruelty because of Jesus are especially blessed. *"Rejoice and be glad,"* he said, *"for your reward is great in heaven."*

Jesus told the people to love their enemies and be good to others, even those who hate them. Jesus taught that it is good to treat others the way we want to be treated. He encouraged the people to depend on God and not to worry about what to eat or what to wear.

He promised that everyone who hears his words and obeys them is like a person who builds their house on a firm foundation. The storms of life will not be able to shake that person. These teachings of Jesus are the new law of love.

THE ROSARY

Third Luminous Mystery

THE PROCLAMATION OF THE KINGDOM

(Matthew 5:1-12)

Jesus Heals the Centurion's Servant

Matthew 8:5-13

Jesus spent a lot of time in the town of Capernaum. In that town was a **synagogue** where he would preach.

There was a Roman soldier in Capernaum who had donated money to build the synagogue. The soldier was a **centurion** in charge of a hundred soldiers who were camped near the town. The centurion had a servant whom he loved very much but who had become sick. The centurion had heard of the miracles and teaching of Jesus, and he believed that Jesus could heal his servant.

The centurion asked Jesus to heal his servant, and Jesus gladly said, "I will come and heal him." The centurion replied, ***"Lord, I am not worthy to have you come under my roof; but only say the word, and my servant will be healed."*** Jesus was impressed by the centurion's faith. He said, "Go. It has been done for you as you believed." And at that moment, the servant was healed.

Jesus Gives His Authority to the Twelve

Luke 9:1-9

Jesus performed many miracles in the region of Capernaum. Then Jesus gave his twelve disciples the authority to go out and heal the sick and free those who are troubled by demons. The disciples are also referred to as **apostles**. Jesus sent them out with power to heal and to proclaim the kingdom of God.

Jesus Feeds the Five Thousand

Luke 9:10-27

Large crowds gathered near the Sea of Galilee outside Capernaum to hear Jesus teach. After a while, they became hungry. The disciples said to Jesus, "Send them away to get food."

Jesus replied, "They don't need to go away. You give them food."

This seemed impossible to the disciples. They only had five loaves of bread and two fish. Jesus said, "Bring the bread and fish to me."

Then Jesus instructed the disciples to have the people sit down in groups. He took the five loaves and two fish, looked up to heaven, said a blessing, and broke the bread. He gave them to the disciples to share.

About five thousand men plus women and children were able to eat until they were full! When the leftovers were gathered up, they filled twelve baskets! This amazing miracle helps us understand how the **Eucharist** feeds the whole Church.

The Transfiguration

Luke 9:28-36

Soon after the feeding of the five thousand, Jesus took Peter, James, and John and climbed a mountain to pray.

While they were on the mountain, Jesus' appearance changed, and his clothes became a shimmering white. Moses and Elijah, the prophets from the Old Testament, appeared, standing next to him and speaking to him.

The disciples were afraid when a cloud overshadowed them, but the voice of God came from the cloud. He said, *"This is my Son, my Chosen; listen to him!"* Once again, God confirmed that Jesus is the Son of God.

What do you think?

1. What was the result of Mary saying "yes" to God's plan for her?
2. How do you know that Jesus is divine?
3. How do you create personal time to listen to God?

HE WENT ON HIS WAY THROUGH TOWNS AND VILLAGES, TEACHING, AND JOURNEYING TOWARD JERUSALEM.

—Luke 13:22

Chapter Nineteen

Jesus Teaches About the Kingdom of God

Luke

Jesus taught throughout the region of Galilee. As he connected with people, he assured them of God's love and encouraged them to show God's love and mercy to one another. Jesus also teaches us how to be holy, as God is holy. Through him we have a relationship with God, our Father. When we follow God's law, we are witnesses to his kingdom here on earth.

Bible Reading Checklist

- [ ] LUKE 10:1-12; 25–37 Jesus appoints the seventy; parable of the Good Samaritan
- [ ] LUKE 11:1-13; MATTHEW 6:9-13; LUKE 13:18-21 The Our Father; Jesus tells kingdom parables
- [ ] MATTHEW 16:13-28; LUKE 13:31-35 Peter's confession of faith; Jesus in danger
- [ ] LUKE 15; 17:11-21; 18:15-17 Parables of the lost; Jesus heals ten lepers; Jesus welcomes the children
- [ ] LUKE 18:31-34; 19:1-10; MATTHEW 20:29-34 Jesus predicts his passion; Jesus meets Zacchaeus; Jesus heals blind men in Jericho

Jesus Appoints the Seventy

Luke 10:1-12

In addition to the twelve apostles, many people began to follow Jesus. Of these, Jesus chose seventy helpers and sent them out in pairs to go into the towns ahead. Jesus wanted his followers to spread the good news of the gospel, so he told them, *"The harvest is plenty, but laborers are few."* Jesus instructed the helpers not to bring any money or to pack any bags. They would be relying only on God! They would bring peace to the homes that offered them a place to rest. However, if a town did not welcome them, Jesus told them to "Remove your sandals and shake off the dust!" He gave them the power to heal the sick and to save people from evil spirits.

EVIL SPIRITS

"Evil spirits" refers to the fallen angels we read about in Chapter Two. Satan convinced some other angels to follow him. These evil spirits are called demons (see 2 Peter 2:4; 1 John 3:8; John 8:44; CCC 391-395). Demons are enemies who try to harm us by drawing us away from God. We do not have to be afraid of them, because God protects us and gives us the strength to resist their temptations (see Mark 1:27, 6:7; 1 John 4:4; CCC 447).

The Parable of the Good Samaritan

Luke 10:25-37

One of the **scribes** asked Jesus how he could gain eternal life. Jesus asked him, "What is written in the law of Moses?" The scribe said, "We are to love the Lord God with all our heart, all our soul, all our strength, and all our mind. We are also to love our neighbors as ourselves" (Deuteronomy 6:4-5; Leviticus 19:18).

Jesus told the scribe, "You are right. Do this and you will live."

Then the scribe asked Jesus, "But who is my neighbor?"

Jesus answered him by telling a parable, or story. He said there was a poor Jewish man who was beaten, robbed, and left lying in the middle of the road. Several of his countrymen passed by and saw him, but they did not stop to help him. Then a Samaritan (a foreigner) saw him and picked him up off the road. He treated his wounds and brought him to an inn where he would be cared for. He paid what was needed and promised to come back to make sure the man was all right.

Then Jesus said to the scribe, "Who acted like a neighbor in this story?" The scribe answered, "The one who helped him." Jesus replied, "Yes, now you go and do the same."

The Our Father

Luke 11:1-13; Matthew 6:9-13

Jesus prayed every day, and his disciples saw this. One day, they said to him, "Lord, teach us to pray."

Jesus wanted them to understand that God is our Father and we are his children. Jesus said to them, "When you pray, say, *'Father, hallowed be your name. Your kingdom come. Give us each day our daily bread; and forgive us our sins, for we ourselves forgive everyone who is indebted to us; and lead us not into temptation.'*"

The words of the prayer found in Matthew's Gospel are the familiar ***"Our Father"*** that we say at every Mass.

Jesus went on to teach his disciples to persevere in prayer and to trust that the Father wants to give them all good things.

Jesus Tells Kingdom Parables

Luke 13:18-21

Jesus told the disciples many stories, or parables, about what the kingdom of God is like.

In one parable, he said that the kingdom is like a tiny mustard seed. The seed grows into such a large tree that all kinds of birds can make nests in it. In another parable, he said that the kingdom is like leaven, or yeast, that goes into bread dough to make it rise.

Jesus wanted everyone to know that the kingdom of God is growing, and everyone is invited to be a part of it.

Peter's Confession of Faith

Matthew 16:13-28

Jesus took his disciples to a city called Caesarea Philippi, which is built near a large rock cliff. He asked his disciples, *"Who do people say the **Son of Man** is?"*

They responded, "Some say John the Baptist, Elijah, Jeremiah, or another prophet."

Then Jesus asked, *"But who do you say that I am?"*

Simon Peter said, *"You are the Christ, the Son of the living God."* By calling Jesus "the **Christ**," Peter was saying he knew that Jesus is God's anointed one, or Messiah, who has come to save the world.

After Peter's declaration of faith, Jesus said, *"Blessed are you! My father in heaven has revealed this to you. You are Peter, and on this rock, I will build my church."* The name *Peter* means "rock." Jesus put Peter in charge of the Church that He would build. He gave Peter the keys to the kingdom, which means Peter would be the first **pope**, the person who leads the Church (see CCC 880-882).

Jesus in Danger

Luke 13:31-35

While Jesus was teaching about the kingdom of God, he knew that some people did not like what he taught.

Many of the Jewish leaders were afraid that his teachings would lead people away from their ways of worship. Others feared that if Jesus really was a king, then the Roman Empire would punish the people, because Caesar wanted to be the only king.

A group of **Pharisees** came to Jesus to tell him that King Herod Antipas wanted to kill him. Jesus was not afraid. He told the Pharisees, "Many prophets have been killed in Jerusalem for speaking the truth."

Jesus knew that he would be killed in Jerusalem like the prophets before him. Even so, he wanted the people of Jerusalem to receive his love.

Parables of the Lost

Luke 15

God loves each and every soul. God will not abandon any of us. To help us understand how important we are to God, Jesus told some parables about things that were lost and then found again.

The first story was about a lost sheep. The shepherd left his ninety-nine other sheep to find the one that was lost. When he found it, he carried it home on his shoulders, singing for joy. He was very happy!

The second story was about a lost coin. A woman had ten coins and lost one. She searched for it high and low. When she finally found it, she was so happy that she asked all her friends and neighbors to celebrate with her.

Jesus also told a story about a man who had two sons. The younger son took his full share of the property and moved away from home. He wasted all the money on parties and things that didn't matter in an extravagant, **prodigal** way. He became so poor that even the food that was given to pigs looked better than what he had to eat.

Feeling sorry for himself and ashamed of his actions, he went home to his father. When his father saw him coming, he shouted for joy! The father ran out to greet his son.

"Father, I have sinned," the son said. "I am not worthy to be called your son."

But the father was full of mercy. He welcomed his son, telling his servants, "Let's celebrate! *For my son was lost, but now he is found!*"

The older brother was jealous about the party given for his brother. He didn't think his brother deserved it. His father assured his older son that he loved him, too. He told him that he was rejoicing because his lost son had been found. God is like the happy father who welcomes us when we come to him.

Jesus Heals Ten Lepers

Luke 17:11-21

As Jesus journeyed toward Jerusalem for the Feast of Passover, he met a group of **lepers.** Lepers were not allowed to be with other people because of their disease. The ten lepers cried out to Jesus for mercy, and Jesus healed them. Then he told them to show themselves to a priest to be declared "clean" from the disease.

Although ten were healed, only one turned back to thank Jesus for his kindness. The one who returned to him was a Samaritan and not a Jew.

Jesus asked him, "Where are the other nine?" Jesus was surprised that his own people did not thank him for being healed.

Jesus continued to preach about the Kingdom of God to show that it is in our midst.

Jesus Welcomes the Children

Luke 18:15-17

Many of the people who came to Jesus brought their babies and children with them. They wanted Jesus to bless them.

The disciples scolded the people, but Jesus welcomed them all. Jesus said, *"Let the children come to me, for the kingdom of God belongs to such as these."*

The kingdom of God belongs to everyone who trusts God and accepts his love as children do.

Jesus Predicts His Passion

Luke 18:31-34

At times, Jesus spoke privately with his twelve disciples. As they traveled toward Jerusalem for the Feast of the Passover, he told them what would happen. Jesus said, "Everything that is written about me will be accomplished" (see Isaiah 53).

He told them that the Son of Man (see Daniel 7:14) would be beaten and killed but would rise from the dead on the third day. Jesus' bodily suffering, death on a cross, and resurrection are known as his **passion.**

The disciples did not understand what Jesus was trying to tell them. They thought that the Messiah would free the Jews from the Roman government. They thought he would lead them as King David had done many years before. They hoped Jesus would become an earthly king.

Jesus Meets Zacchaeus

Luke 19:1-10

As Jesus and his disciples continued toward Jerusalem, they passed through the town of Jericho. A crowd gathered around him there.

There was a tax collector in the crowd named Zacchaeus. He had become very wealthy by cheating people when he collected their taxes.

Zacchaeus wanted to see Jesus, but he was too short to see him over the heads of the people. Zacchaeus ran ahead of the crowd and climbed a sycamore tree. He was surprised when Jesus stopped by the tree and looked up at him.

Jesus said, "Zacchaeus, come down! I'll stay at your house tonight."

Zacchaeus was overjoyed, but some people in the crowd grumbled. They didn't think Jesus should spend time with such a sinner.

Because of Jesus' love, Zacchaeus became a changed man. He repented of his sins and returned the money he had gained dishonestly. He also gave money to the poor.

Jesus called Zacchaeus a "true son of Abraham," which meant that Zacchaeus now had a heart to follow God. He was living the way God wants all his children to live, with a generous, repentant heart, able to care for others. Through his repentance, Zacchaeus received the promise of salvation—the same promise that was made to Abraham, the father of the Jewish people, thousands of years before.

Jesus Heals Blind Men in Jericho

Matthew 20:29-34

As Jesus left Jericho, a crowd continued to follow him. They passed two blind men sitting by the roadside, who kept calling out to Jesus asking to be healed. The people in the crowd told the blind men to be quiet, but they cried out even louder, saying, ***"Have mercy on us,*** Son of David!"

Jesus asked, "What do you want me to do for you?"

They replied, "Lord, let our eyes be opened."

Feeling pity for the men, he touched their eyes, and they could see again!

When he reached Jerusalem, Jesus was ready for the last days of his earthly life. He had chosen twelve men to carry on his mission after he was no longer with them. Jesus had taught his followers well by the way he lived his life and what he said. He demonstrated how his followers could bring healing, truth, and love to the world.

What do you think?

1. Do you have a favorite parable that Jesus told? What is it, and why do you like it?
2. Can you say the "Our Father"? What does Jesus teach us about forgiveness in this prayer?
3. Describe what it might be like to sit in the lap of Jesus and listen to him tell stories.

"AND HE TOOK BREAD, AND WHEN HE HAD GIVEN THANKS HE BROKE IT AND GAVE IT TO THEM, SAYING, 'THIS IS MY BODY WHICH IS GIVEN FOR YOU. DO THIS IN REMEMBRANCE OF ME.'"

—Luke 22:19

Chapter Twenty

Jesus Establishes the New Covenant

Luke

Jesus and his apostles return to Jerusalem to celebrate the Jewish festival of Passover. Jesus is greeted with praise and cries of "Hosanna." After sharing his body and blood with the apostles at the Last Supper, Jesus is betrayed by Judas and arrested. Even though he is innocent, he accepts death on the cross to pay the price for all of our sins. Our relationship with God is restored as Jesus shows us the way to share eternal life with him in heaven.

Bible Reading Checklist

- [ ] **LUKE 19:28-48** Jesus' triumphal entry into Jerusalem
- [ ] **LUKE 22:1-62; JOHN 13:3-16** The Last Supper; the Garden of Gethsemane
- [ ] **LUKE 22:63–24:12; JOHN 19:25-27** Jesus' passion, death, and resurrection
- [ ] **LUKE 24:13-49; JOHN 20:19-29** The risen Lord on the road to Emmaus; Jesus breathes on the disciples; Thomas comes to believe in the Resurrection
- [ ] **LUKE 24:50-53; MATTHEW 28:18-20** The Great Commission and The Ascension

Jesus' Triumphal Entry into Jerusalem

Luke 19:28-48

When Jesus arrived for the last time in Jerusalem, he rode a humble donkey into the city. The people put their coats on the road to carpet the path. They were excited to see him and shouted, ***"Blessed is he who comes in the name of the Lord! Hosanna in the highest!"*** (Matthew 21:9; Luke 19:38). We repeat these words at Mass during the Eucharistic prayer. We also recite, ***"Holy, holy, holy is the LORD of hosts; the whole earth is full of his glory"*** (Isaiah 6:3).

Although the people of Jerusalem were excited about Jesus' arrival, Jesus wept as he looked over the city. He talked about a time to come when the city and the Temple would be destroyed.

When Jesus got off the donkey near the Temple, he saw crowds of people. They were selling things at high prices, treating the Temple as a marketplace instead of the holy house of God.

This made Jesus angry. He drove them out, saying, *"It is written, 'My house shall be a house of prayer' but you have made it a den of robbers!"* (Luke 19:46).

Every day he taught in the Temple, but not everyone in Jerusalem wanted to listen to his teachings. Some people wanted to trick him so that he would say something against the Roman government. Then they could have him arrested.

SACRAMENT
OF THE
HOLY EUCHARIST

SACRAMENT
OF
HOLY ORDERS

The Last Supper

Luke 22:1-38; John 13:3-16

While Jesus was in Jerusalem, the Feast of Passover arrived. The Passover meal recalls the deliverance of the Jewish people from slavery in Egypt, as told in the book of Exodus. The Israelites were saved from the angel of death by the blood of the lamb, which was painted on their doorposts.

Jesus and his twelve apostles were together to celebrate the feast. During Jesus' celebration of the Passover meal, he told his disciples the new meaning of the Passover. He told them that his own blood would be shed for a new kind of deliverance.

He took a cup of wine, and when he had given thanks, he said, *"Take this, and divide it among yourselves; for I tell you that from now on I shall not drink of the fruit of the vine until the kingdom of God comes"* (Luke 22:17-18).

Then Jesus took bread, and when he had given thanks, he broke it and gave it to his disciples, saying, ***"This is my body which is given for you. Do this in remembrance of me"*** (Luke 22:19). And after dinner he took the cup, telling his disciples that the cup is the new covenant in his blood, which would be shed for many. Secretly, before the meal, Judas had made plans to betray

Jesus to the Jewish leaders. Judas left the supper before it was finished.

Jesus reminded them that the one who serves others is the greater one. He demonstrated this to them by washing their feet. As servants of the Lord they would be called to do the same. During the rest of the meal the disciples began arguing about who was the greatest. Jesus specifically told Peter that he would deny him three times before the cock crowed the next day.

THE ROSARY

Fifth Luminous Mystery

THE INSTITUTION OF THE EUCHARIST

(Luke 22:19-20)

The Garden of Gethsemane

Luke 22:39-62

After they had eaten, Jesus and his disciples went to the Garden of Gethsemane to pray. This garden is on the Mount of Olives in Jerusalem.

Jesus was very troubled knowing that soon he would suffer in great agony for the sins of the world. His sweat became like drops of blood falling to the ground. He prayed, "Father, if you are willing, take this from me. Nevertheless, not my will, but yours be done!"

Then he got up and found that his disciples had fallen asleep. He said to them, *"Why do you sleep? Rise and pray that you don't fall into temptation"* (Luke 22:46).

Now a crowd arrived at the garden, led by Judas Iscariot who gave Jesus a kiss. Then the chief priests and Temple guards arrested Jesus and took him away, even though he was innocent, just like the lamb that was sacrificed for the Passover meal.

While Jesus was betrayed, Peter followed at a distance. He was questioned by those around him, who asked, "Weren't you with Jesus?" Peter quickly replied, "I don't know who you're talking about." In this way, Peter denied knowing Christ three times before a morning cock crowed. Peter remembered Jesus' prediction from the night before, and he wept bitterly.

Jesus' Passion

Luke 22:63-23:43

The Jewish leaders held a secret trial in the middle of the night. They said to Jesus, *"If you are the Christ, tell us"* (Luke 22:67).

Jesus replied, "If I tell you, you will not believe."

They asked, "Are you the Son of God, then?"

Jesus replied, *"You say that I am"* (Luke 22:70).

They became very angry and brought Jesus to Pontius Pilate, the Roman governor of Judea. Pilate asked him, "Are you the king of the Jews?"

Jesus answered, *"You have said so"* (Luke 23:3).

Pilate then sent him to Herod, another Roman governor. Herod's men put a royal robe on Jesus, mocking him. Then Herod sent him back to Pilate.

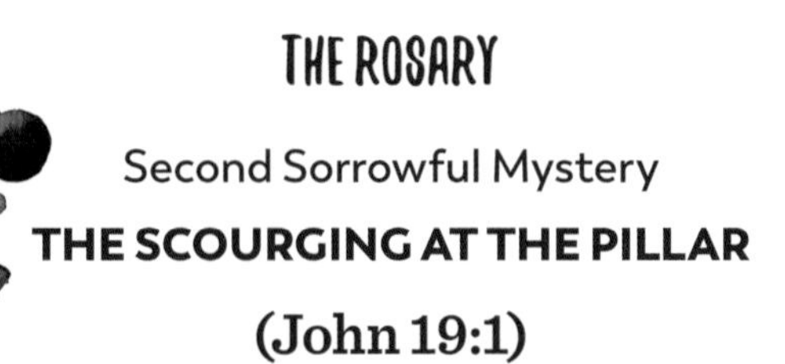

THE ROSARY

Third Sorrowful Mystery

THE CROWNING WITH THORNS

(Matthew 27:28-29)

Pilate said, "We find no fault in Jesus. I will have him whipped, and then I will release him." So the Roman guards whipped him. They placed a crown of thorns on his head (see Matthew 27:29-30). The crowds yelled, "Crucify him!"

Pilate gave in to their demand. He ordered his soldiers to crucify Jesus. They made Jesus carry a cross of wood to a rocky hill outside the city of Jerusalem. There, Jesus was nailed to the Cross and left to die, along with two criminals.

One of the crucified criminals joined the soldiers who mocked Jesus. The other criminal recognized that Jesus was the Son of God. He said, "Jesus, remember me when you come into your kingdom."

Jesus replied, *"Today, you will be with me in Paradise"* (Luke 23:43).

Jesus' Death

Luke 23:44-56; John 19:25-27

Along with the apostle John, there were some women standing under the Cross near Jesus. They were Mary Magdalene, Mary the wife of Clopas, and Mary the mother of Jesus.

It was very hard for Jesus' mother to see him suffer, but she trusted God. When Jesus saw her there with the apostle John, he said to her, "Woman, behold, your son." Then he said to John, "Behold, your mother." He did this to give his mother to all who believe in him as John did. John took care of Mary from that moment on.

THE ROSARY

Fourth Sorrowful Mystery

JESUS CARRIES THE CROSS

(Luke 23:44-56; John 19:25-27)

THE ROSARY

Fifth Sorrowful Mystery

THE CRUCIFIXION

(Luke 23:46)

THE SIXTH COVENANT: ONE HOLY CHURCH

Jesus establishes the New Covenant by dying on the Cross for our sins, then rising again and ascending into heaven. The New Covenant family of God is the body of Christ, One Holy Church.

At about three o'clock in the afternoon, Jesus cried out in a loud voice, *"Father, into your hands I commit my spirit"* (Luke 23:46). Then Jesus died. At that moment the earth shook (see Matthew 27:51), and the **veil of the Temple** ripped in two.

We remember the day that Jesus died as Good Friday. This day is only "good" because of the events that happened next. Jesus was buried in a tomb with a large rock covering the entrance, but his story wasn't over.

Jesus' Resurrection

Luke 24:1-12

On Sunday, the third day after Jesus was buried, Mary Magdalene and several other women went to the tomb. They were alarmed to find that the large stone had been rolled away.

They looked into the tomb and found that Jesus' body was not there! An angel appeared to them. He said, *"Why do you seek the living among the dead? He is not here, but has risen!"* (Luke 24:5).

Then the women remembered what Jesus had said before he died. They ran quickly to tell the apostles that the tomb was empty!

The news of Jesus' resurrection is the long-awaited Good News that God promised Eve in Genesis 3:15, that her offspring would conquer sin and death. The Resurrection is the "crowning truth of our Faith" (CCC 638). It gives us hope that we, too, will be raised to eternal life (see CCC 658).

"For our sake he was crucified
under Pontius Pilate,
he suffered death and was buried."

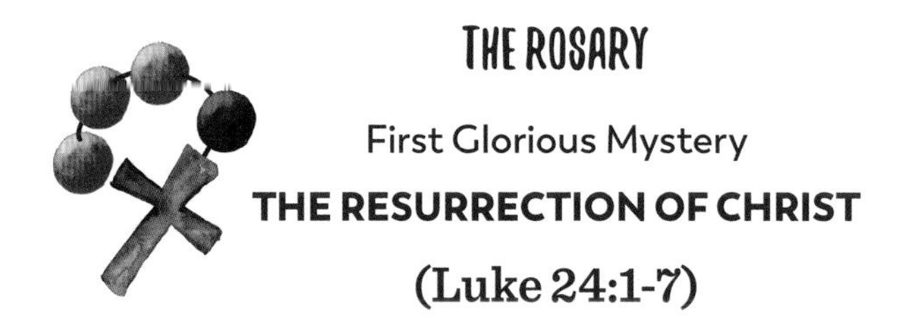

THE ROSARY

First Glorious Mystery

THE RESURRECTION OF CHRIST

(Luke 24:1-7)

The Risen Lord on the Road to Emmaus

Luke 24:13-49

On that same Easter day, Jesus appeared to two disciples walking on the road to a town called Emmaus. They did not recognize him as they walked along telling him sadly about all that had happened to Jesus.

They heard that the tomb was empty, but they did not know how that could happen. Jesus then explained how the stories of Moses and the prophets pointed to the Messiah and why the Messiah had to suffer.

As they approached a village, the disciples invited the stranger to come in to eat with them. Jesus joined them for supper. During the meal he took the bread, blessed it, broke it, and gave it to them. At that moment the disciples recognized him.

Then Jesus vanished from their sight. They said, *"Didn't our hearts burn while he talked about the Scriptures with us?"* They were so filled with joy that they ran all the way back to Jerusalem to share with the disciples what had happened. They cried, *"The Lord is risen indeed!"* (see Luke 24:14).

We can feel that same joy today when we share in the Eucharistic meal. Jesus is with us each time we receive his Body, Blood, Soul, and Divinity under the appearance of bread and wine at Mass.

Jesus Breathes on the Disciples; Thomas Comes to Believe in the Resurrection

John 20:19-29

Also on Easter, many of the disciples were gathered together in an upper room in Jerusalem when Jesus came to them.

They were frightened at first, but Jesus reassured them, saying, "***Peace be with you***" (John 20:19). Then he breathed on them, giving them the Holy Spirit.

He told them that any sins they forgave would also be forgiven by God, and any sins they did not forgive would not be forgiven by God. This authority that Jesus gave to the apostles has been passed on to priests for the sacrament of reconciliation.

Thomas was not with the apostles when Jesus appeared to them, and when he heard about it, he did not believe it. He said he would only believe if he could actually touch the wounds in Jesus' hands and side.

Eight days later, the apostles were in the upper room again when Jesus suddenly appeared. Jesus said to Thomas, "Put your finger here and see my hands. Feel the wound in my side."

Thomas believed, saying, "*My Lord and my God!*" (John 20:28). Then Jesus told them that people who believe without seeing are blessed. We have not seen Jesus with our own eyes, yet we are blessed because we believe through faith.

The Great Commission and the Ascension

Luke 24:50-53; Matthew 28:18-20

Over forty days, Jesus appeared to his disciples many times and continued to teach them. He told them to stay in Jerusalem until the Holy Spirit came to fill them with power.

Then Jesus brought his disciples to Bethany, a town outside Jerusalem.

Jesus blessed them and said, *"Go therefore and make disciples of all nations, baptizing them in the name of the Father and of the Son and of the Holy Spirit, teaching them to observe all that I have commanded you; and behold, I am with you always, to the close of the age."* (Matthew 28:18-20).

As he blessed them, Jesus was carried up into heaven to be with his Father. He rose higher and higher, as if he were on a cloud, until he was out of sight. Although the disciples did not want Jesus to leave, they were full of joy. They understood that Jesus would live through them as they shared his love with others.

THE ROSARY

Second Glorious Mystery

THE ASCENSION

(Luke 24:51)

"He ascended into heaven and is seated at the right hand of the Father."

THE GREAT COMMISSION

And Jesus came and said to them, *"All authority in heaven and on earth has been given to me. Go therefore and make disciples of all nations, baptizing them in the name of the Father and of the Son and of the Holy Spirit, teaching them to observe all that I have commanded you; and behold, I am with you always, to the close of the age."*

—Matthew 28:18-20

What do you think?

1. Do you get angry sometimes? How can you be angry and not sin?
2. How do you share in Jesus' suffering on the cross?
3. How would you recognize Jesus if he walked alongside you today?

WHEN THE DAY OF PENTECOST HAD COME, THEY WERE ALL TOGETHER IN ONE PLACE.

—Acts 2:1

Chapter Twenty-One

The Holy Spirit Ignites the Church

Acts

The Holy Spirit came upon the disciples of Jesus at Pentecost, giving them the strength they needed to be witnesses to the Gospel. There were three waves, or movements, that established the Church. Here, in the first wave, Peter, James, John, and Stephen shared the story of Jesus in Jerusalem. Stephen became the first martyr to die for his faith in Jesus.

Bible Reading Checklist

- [ ] ACTS 1 Matthias replaces Judas
- [ ] ACTS 2 The day of Pentecost
- [ ] ACTS 3:1-16; 4:1-22, 32-37 Peter and John heal a lame man; the Church shares
- [ ] ACTS 5:12-42 The disciples witness to the Jewish leaders
- [ ] ACTS 6–8:3 The martyrdom of Stephen

Matthias Replaces Judas

Acts 1

After Jesus' ascension, the apostles returned to the upper room with Mary, Jesus' mother, and the other women. Since Judas Iscariot had left them, the remaining eleven apostles prayed that God would show them who should take his place as one of the Twelve. They chose a man named Matthias to take his position. Matthias had followed Jesus as a disciple throughout his ministry.

The Day of Pentecost

Acts 2

The apostles were in Jerusalem for the Feast of Pentecost. Pentecost was celebrated fifty days after Passover. The apostles were expecting something to happen because Jesus had told them to wait there, in Jerusalem, for the Holy Spirit.

Suddenly, when they were all together, they heard a rushing sound like the wind, and tongues of fire appeared over their heads. Then they began to speak in languages that they hadn't learned before.

They were so excited they rushed out into the streets! They spoke to the Jewish pilgrims who were visiting Jerusalem from other countries. The people were surprised and asked, "How is it that we each hear them speaking in our own language?" This dramatic experience was a fulfillment of prophecy spoken by the prophet Joel: "I will pour out my spirit on all flesh" (Joel 2:28).

Thousands of people believed in Jesus through the apostles' preaching of the gospel that day. They were baptized outside the Temple in the purification pools near the main steps. Modern archaeologists have uncovered these pools and steps, which can still be seen today. The day of Pentecost is considered the birthday of the Church (see CCC 2623).

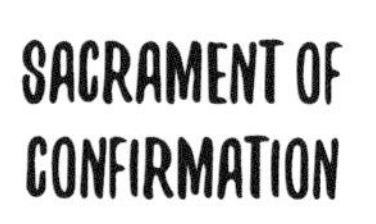

"I believe in the Holy Spirit,
the Lord, the giver of life,
who proceeds from the Father and the Son,
who with the Father and the Son is adored and glorified,
who has spoken through the prophets."

THE ROSARY

Third Glorious Mystery

THE DESCENT OF THE HOLY SPIRIT

(Acts 2:4)

Peter and John Heal a Lame Man

Acts 3:1-16; 4:1-22

On their way to the Temple, Peter and John met a lame man begging. Peter said, *"I don't have silver or gold, but what I have I will give you. In the name of Jesus Christ of Nazareth, walk!"* (Acts 3:6). Then Peter took him by the hand and helped him stand up. The man was healed and began leaping about and praising God.

A big crowd came to see what happened, and they were astounded! Peter spoke to them about Jesus Christ.

Some of the priests and **Sadducees** were angry when Peter and John began to preach about Jesus' resurrection, because they didn't believe it had happened. They had Peter and John arrested. But many people had already become believers in Christ because of what they had heard and seen that day—five thousand in all.

Peter and John were brought before Annas the high priest and Caiaphas. They asked, "By whose name have you done this?" Peter was filled with the Holy Spirit. He answered, *"The lame man was healed by the power and name of Jesus Christ of Nazareth, whom you crucified and whom God raised from the dead!"* (Acts 4:10).

The Jewish leaders let them go, but they warned Peter and John not to speak about Jesus again. Peter and John went back to the other disciples. Together they prayed for courage to speak the truth about Jesus.

The Church Shares

Acts 4:32-37

The believers shared everything with each other. They cheerfully gave all they had to God to support the work of spreading the Good News of Jesus Christ. They sold their property and shared the money with the others.

Many people came to hear the disciples preach and to witness God's healing power. When the disciples prayed and laid their hands on people, God healed them. The Church began to grow in numbers as thousands of people believed and were baptized and filled with the Holy Spirit.

The Disciples Witness to the Jewish Leaders

Acts 5:12-42

Many people were now following the gospel of Christ. This made the high priest and religious leaders angry and jealous of the disciples' work. They arrested them and put them in jail, but the disciples escaped with the help of the Holy Spirit.

The disciples went to the Temple and began preaching to the people again. The religious leaders said, "We told you not to teach in the name of Jesus, but you keep doing it!"

Peter said, "We must obey God rather than men."

Then one of the leaders, named **Gamaliel,** spoke up. He told the others that this might be the work of God, so the leaders should not stop it. They let the disciples go.

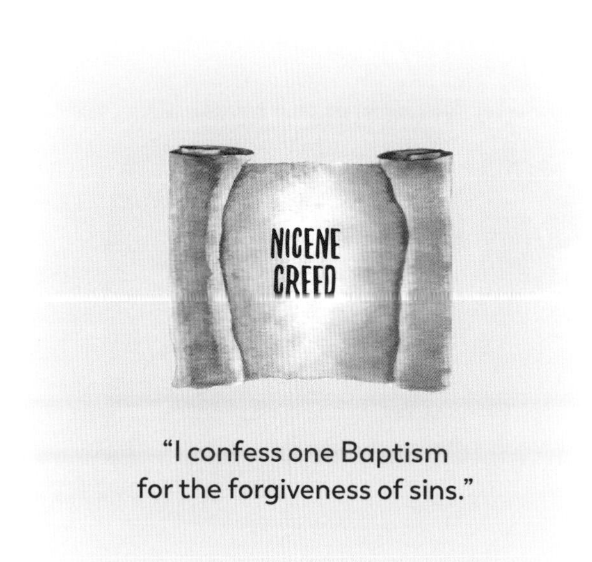

"I confess one Baptism for the forgiveness of sins."

The Martyrdom of Stephen

Acts 6–8:3

So many people were becoming believers in Jesus Christ that the disciples needed to appoint men to help them. They chose seven men who had good reputations and were wise and full of the Holy Spirit. The apostles laid their hands on them and prayed over them, naming them **deacons.** One of the new deacons was Stephen, who was full of grace and power and spoke with great wisdom.

The religious leaders continued to object to the preaching of the gospel. They had Stephen arrested, accusing him of breaking the Law of Moses.

Stephen was brave and trusted God to help him speak the truth. He told the high priest and everyone gathered there about God's plan of salvation through Jesus Christ, but this only made them angrier. Stephen looked up and said, "I see the heavens opened and the Son of Man standing at the right hand of God!"

They shouted and crowded around Stephen, dragging him out of the city to stone him. As he died, Stephen prayed, *"Lord, do not hold this sin against them"* (Acts 7:60). In this way, Stephen became the first Christian martyr because he was killed for believing in Jesus.

A Jewish leader named Saul was watching as Stephen was stoned and approved of it. Saul persecuted those who believed in Jesus. He went from house to house, arresting men and women and throwing them in jail for their faith.

What do you think?

1. What does it mean that the Holy Spirit dwells in you because of your baptism?
2. What are some ways that you share with others?
3. How can you act like Jesus so others can see him in you?

NOW THOSE WHO WERE SCATTERED WENT ABOUT PREACHING THE WORD.

—Acts 8:4

Chapter Twenty-Two

The Apostles Spread the Gospel

Acts

The Church continued to grow. In a second wave of witnessing, the Good News, or gospel, was shared in the territory of Judea and Samaria. Saul was converted and came to believe in Jesus. His name was changed to Paul. He spent the rest of his life building the Church. God revealed to Peter that everyone in the world is welcome in the Church. With this event, God's promise to Abraham of a worldwide blessing was fulfilled.

Bible Reading Checklist

- [ ] **ACTS 8:4-40 The apostles spread the gospel**
- [ ] **ACTS 9:1-25 The conversion of Saul**
- [ ] **ACTS 10; 11:19-26 Peter's vision of the unclean animals; the first Christians**
- [ ] **ACTS 12:1-19; 13:13-43 Peter's arrest and deliverance; Paul's first missionary journey**
- [ ] **ACTS 15:1-21 Council at Jerusalem**

The Apostles Spread the Gospel

Acts 8:4-40

The apostles spread out from Jerusalem to preach the gospel in other cities. One of the new deacons, named Philip, went to the city of Samaria and told the people about Jesus the Messiah. Through Philip, God healed many who were sick or possessed by **unclean spirits**.

People were eager to be baptized when they heard the Good News. They believed that Jesus was the Messiah and that God wanted them to turn away from sin and be healed. Peter and John laid hands on them so that they could also receive the Holy Spirit. This is the same way that we receive the sacrament of Confirmation today.

When Philip left Samaria, he traveled a road that goes from Jerusalem to Gaza. On the way, he met a **eunuch** who worked for the queen of **Ethiopia**. The eunuch had been in Jerusalem to worship and was on his way back to Ethiopia. He was reading the prophet Isaiah and asked Philip to explain a passage.

Philip told him how Jesus fulfilled the things written in the Old Testament Scriptures. The eunuch understood that Jesus is the Messiah. He said excitedly, *"See, here is some water! What is stopping me from getting baptized?"* (Acts 8:36). Philip baptized him then and there, and the eunuch went away rejoicing.

The Conversion of Saul

Acts 9:1-25

Saul was still arresting people who believed in Jesus Christ. He had encouraged the people to kill Stephen. Now he was on his way to Damascus to arrest more believers.

As he was traveling, Saul was suddenly surrounded by a shining bright light from heaven. Saul fell to the ground. He heard a voice call, "Saul, Saul, why do you persecute me?"

Saul cried out, "Who are you, Lord?"

The voice replied, *"I am Jesus, whom you are persecuting. Get up and go into the city. There you will be told what to do"* (Acts 9:4-6).

Saul understood that he had been attacking Jesus himself and hurting his Church. He was sorry and decided to follow Jesus. As Saul got up, he realized he was blind. His friends helped him find his way into town.

God called a disciple named Ananias. He said, "Rise and go to a man named Saul. Lay your hands on him so that he can see again."

At first, Ananias did not want to go and heal Saul. Saul had treated the believers cruelly. God said to him, *"Go, for I have chosen him to preach to the* ***Gentiles****, kings, and sons of Israel"* (Acts 9:15).

Ananias went to Saul and laid hands on him. Instantly, Saul was healed of his blindness and filled with the Holy Spirit. Saul was so amazed that he got up right away and wanted to be baptized.

After Saul's conversion, his name was changed to Paul. He became a powerful teacher who convinced many people that Jesus was the Messiah.

Later, Paul went to stay with a group of disciples in the city of Antioch. They gathered together to worship God and preach the gospel of Jesus the Messiah.

Peter's Vision of the Unclean Animals

Acts 10

A centurion named Cornelius lived in the town of Caesarea. Although he wasn't Jewish, he loved God, lived a prayerful life, and helped others.

People who are not Jewish are called Gentiles. Gentiles did not practice circumcision or observe the dietary rules of the Law of Moses. The Jewish people considered Gentiles unclean.

One day as Cornelius prayed, an angel came to tell him that God had heard his prayers. He should send some men to the town of Joppa to ask Peter to come to his house. So Cornelius sent three men to invite Peter to come.

Meanwhile, in the town of Joppa, Peter had a vision. He saw a large sheet lowered from heaven in front of him. There were all kinds of animals on the sheet. Some of the animals were those that Jews were not allowed to eat, because they were considered unclean according to the Law of Moses. In the dream, a voice said to Peter, "Rise and eat the meat of any of the animals."

Peter said, "No, Lord, I have never eaten meat from unclean animals."

The voice replied, *"What God has cleansed, you must not call unclean"* (Acts 10:14).

Peter wondered what this meant. Just then, the men that Cornelius sent came asking for Peter. Peter went with them to Cornelius' house. He saw that Cornelius had faith in God even though he was a Gentile. Then Peter understood what his dream meant: God wanted the Good News about Jesus to be shared with the Gentiles, not just the Jews.

Peter told Cornelius and his household all about Jesus. Everyone who believed was baptized and filled with the Holy Spirit. Peter went back to the Church at Jerusalem and told everyone what had happened. They praised God that his plan of eternal life also included the Gentiles. God's promise to Abraham of a worldwide blessing was fulfilled.

The First Christians

Acts 11:19-26

Peter and the other apostles welcomed Gentiles into the Church and continued to spread the gospel to all as the Church added a large number of people. The disciples in Antioch were the first people in the Church to be called ***Christians.***

Peter's Arrest and Deliverance

Acts 12:1-19

Herod Agrippa, the king, persecuted the Christians. He arrested Peter and put him in prison. Peter was bound with two chains and locked in a cell.

He had fallen asleep when God sent an angel to him. The angel woke him and said, "Get up quickly!" The chains fell off Peter's wrists. "Follow me," said the angel, and he helped Peter escape.

Peter went straight to the house of Mary, the mother of John (also known as Mark). Several Christians had gathered to pray for him there. Peter told them how God had answered their prayers. Then he went to another place to hide from King Herod's men.

The apostles continued to preach the Good News about Jesus, and more and more people became believers.

Paul's First Missionary Journey

Acts 13:13-43

Paul traveled to many parts of the world. He built up God's Church and spread the Good News of salvation.

His first journey began in the city of Antioch and continued on to the island of Cyprus. From there, Paul went to Pisidia, to another town also called Antioch. He spoke to the Jewish people in the synagogue there.

Paul began by saying, "*Men of Israel, and you that fear God, listen*" (Acts 13:16). Then he talked about the history of salvation. He said that God revealed himself to the Israelites first. God kept his covenant by bringing them into the Promised Land. God gave them King David and the prophets. Then Paul told them that Jesus, a descendant of King David, is the Savior. God sent Jesus Christ into the world to establish a New Covenant.

People believed the Good News when they heard Paul preach.

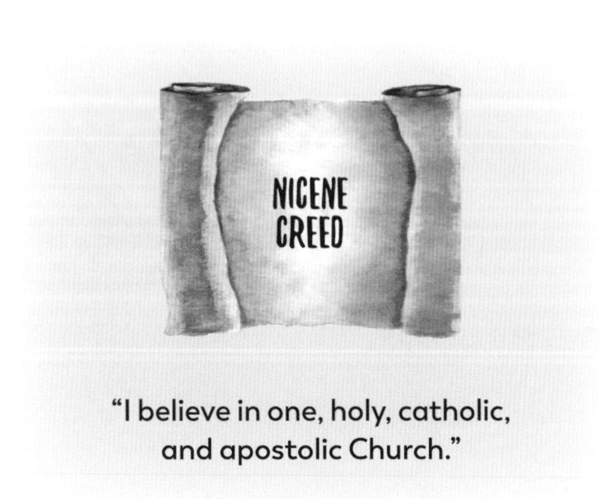

"I believe in one, holy, catholic, and apostolic Church."

Council at Jerusalem

Acts 15:1-21

Many Gentiles wanted to follow the path of Jesus and were baptized. The Jewish people had been trained in the laws of Moses, but Gentiles did not know those laws.

Some Jews thought that the Gentiles needed to obey the old Jewish laws in order to be saved. This was a serious question, and the apostles met in Jerusalem to discuss it.

This meeting, now called the Council of Jerusalem, took place around the year **AD** 50. Paul, Barnabas, Peter, James, and the other apostles prayed and discussed the issue. What laws should Gentiles follow after baptism?

Peter believed that both Jews and Gentiles were saved by the grace of God through Jesus Christ. Gentiles did not have to be circumcised in order to be saved.

Before his crucifixion and resurrection, Jesus gave Peter the "keys to the kingdom" (see Matthew 16:19), the authority to guide the Church. At the council, Peter exercised this authority. He said, *"We shall be saved through the grace of the Lord Jesus, just as they will"* (Acts 15:11). James, who was the bishop of Jerusalem, agreed with him. The council thus determined that Gentiles could be part of the kingdom of God.

The Church has followed the model of the Jerusalem Council. Bishops and priests meet together to clarify matters of faith, guided by the Holy Spirit. The Church has had twenty-one councils in its history. The most recent was the Second Vatican Council, or **Vatican II**, which took place in the 1960s.

What do you think?

1. What is our pope's name, and how does he follow Jesus?
2. How do you think good rules are made?
3. How would you tell someone else about your faith?

SO THE WORD OF THE LORD GREW AND PREVAILED MIGHTILY.

—Acts 19:20

Chapter Twenty-Three

All Are Welcome in the Church

Acts

Paul led a third wave of witnessing. He completed three missionary journeys around the known world to share the Good News of salvation through Jesus Christ.

Bible Reading Checklist

- [ ] ACTS 15:36-41; 16 Paul's second missionary journey
- [ ] ACTS 17–18:11; 19:1-20 Paul continues his journeys
- [ ] ACTS 21:27-40; 22; 26:1-23 Paul's arrest and defense
- [ ] ACTS 27–28:10 Shipwreck on the way to Rome
- [ ] ACTS 28:11-31 Paul in Rome

Optional: *Catechism of the Catholic Church* 966–967 The Assumption of Mary

Paul's Second Missionary Journey

Acts 15:36-41; 16

Inspired by the Holy Spirit, Paul went on a second journey to spread the gospel and to support the new churches. The apostle Barnabas went to the island of Cyprus. Paul and Silas went to the southern region of Asia Minor.

On the way, Paul had a vision. He saw a man from Macedonia inviting him to preach the gospel in that region. So Paul went there, to a city called Philippi, which was part of the country now known as Greece. In Philippi, a woman named Lydia listened to Paul speak about Jesus. Lydia was a merchant who sold purple cloth. Her heart was open to the Word of God, and she asked to be baptized along with everyone in her household.

In the town of Philippi, not everyone was happy with the preaching of Paul and Silas. One day Paul cast out an evil spirit from a slave girl. The leaders of the city put Paul and Silas in prison because of the commotion it caused.

Paul and Silas prayed and sang hymns to God while they were in jail. While they were praying, an earthquake shook the prison. and all the doors flew open. The jailer was afraid that the prisoners would escape, but Paul said, "Do not harm yourself, for we are all still here!"

The jailer was amazed and said, "What must I do to be saved?"

Paul said, *"Believe in the Lord Jesus, and you and your household will be saved"* (Acts 16:28-31).

After this, the city leaders realized that Paul and Silas were Roman citizens, so they released them. Paul continued to spread the gospel throughout Macedonia and Greece.

Paul Continues His Journeys

Acts 17–18:11; 19:1-20

In some communities, like Thessalonica, Paul and his companions were accused of placing Jesus as a rival to Caesar. In other towns, like Beroea, the people were ready to listen to the Word of God. Despite arrests and persecution, the apostles continued to spread the Good News.

Paul continued his journey in Athens and then went on to Corinth. There he stayed with Aquila and his wife, Priscilla. Aquila and Priscilla were Jews who had been expelled from Rome. Aquila and Paul were both tentmakers and practiced their trade together. Priscilla and Aquila welcomed Christians into their home and helped to spread the gospel.

Paul returned to Antioch. Soon he began a third journey to visit many of the regions where he had preached before. He based his work in the city of Ephesus.

The Ephesians had been baptized and were trying to follow God, but they needed the additional strength of the Holy Spirit. Paul laid his hands on them so they could receive the Holy Spirit. Then the Ephesians boldly preached the Word of God throughout Asia.

Paul wrote letters of encouragement to the new churches in the towns he had left. These letters are now part of the New Testament and offer wisdom for us, too. They are known as the epistles, or letters, of Paul.

When Paul wrote to the Philippians at Philippi, he reminded them to be humble, as Christ was humble, and to love others by serving them (see Philippians 2:1-11). Paul encouraged the Thessalonians to *"rejoice always, pray constantly, give thanks in all circumstances; for this is the will of God in Christ Jesus for you"* (1 Thessalonians 5:16-18). In his letter to the Corinthians, Paul wrote, *"There are various gifts, but the same Spirit ... for we were all baptized into one body."* He continued, *"As it is, there are many parts, but just one body"* (1 Corinthians 12:7-31).

Even though we are different, we all have something good to offer. Paul wrote something else, too. He said, "So faith, hope, love abide, these three; but the greatest of these is love."

Paul's Arrest and Defense

Acts 21:27-40; 22; 26:1-23

After three years in Ephesus, Paul returned to Jerusalem, even though the disciples said he would not be safe there. Paul accepted what might happen to him in Jerusalem as the will of God, just as Jesus had done.

As predicted, some Jews in Jerusalem accused Paul of preaching that Jews no longer had to follow their law. They arrested him in Jerusalem and put him on trial.

Then Paul was taken to Caesarea. There the governors Felix and Festus questioned him, followed by King Agrippa. Paul retold his story of growing up as a devout Jew and how he persecuted the first Christians. He talked about his conversion on the road to Damascus. He told King Agrippa about his work for Jesus to proclaim light to the Jews and Gentiles. Because he was a Roman citizen, Paul appealed to Caesar for a fair trial. King Agrippa agreed to let him go, so he was taken by ship to Rome.

Shipwreck on the Way to Rome

Acts 27–28:10

The journey to Rome was long and difficult. It was late in the year and the seas were stormy. At one point the winds became so strong that everyone thought they would die.

That night Paul had a vision. An angel of the Lord told him he was destined to stand before Caesar. Everyone on the ship would survive. The next day Paul told this to the sailors. He said, *"Take heart, men, for I have faith in God"* (Acts 27:25).

The ship was blown by the storm to an island called Malta. Everyone jumped into the sea and swam to the island. Then the ship was broken apart in the waves. The native people greeted them and helped them build a fire and find food.

Suddenly, Paul was bitten by a snake! The natives said, "This man must be a murderer. He has been bitten by a poisonous snake." It was a miracle that Paul did not die. When the natives saw that he was not hurt by the snake, they thought he was a god. Because of this miracle and Paul's preaching, many of the people of the island became believers in Jesus.

Paul in Rome

Acts 28:11-31

Paul and the ship's crew spent the winter on the island of Malta. Then they set sail on another ship. Eventually, Paul arrived in Rome, where he was received warmly by many fellow Christians.

Caesar did not pursue any charges against him, so Paul freely preached the gospel in Rome. He was fulfilling the call of Jesus to go out to the ends of the earth to preach the gospel (see Matthew 28:18-20). Paul was able to teach about Jesus for two more years.

The book of Acts ends here, but the apostles continued to spread the gospel. Eleven of the apostles, as well as Paul, were martyred for their faith. The apostle John was exiled to the island of Patmos. There he had the visions described in the book of Revelation, the last book of the Bible.

The apostles' message continues to be spread throughout the world through the work of the Church. We too have heard the Good News, and it is up to us to tell others!

The Assumption of Mary

Catechism of the Catholic Church 966–967

When her life on earth came to an end, the Blessed Virgin Mary's body and soul was assumed, or taken up, into heaven by God. We know that Mary was faithful to God, and so her body was brought to heaven as one of the first fruits of the resurrection of her son, Jesus (see 1 Corinthians 15:20). Her **assumption** gives all Christians hope of what God has in store for them. Mary is a gift to the Church as our Mother. She is our helper on the journey to heaven by her **intercession**.

THE ROSARY

Fourth Glorious Mystery

THE ASSUMPTION OF MARY INTO HEAVEN

"There is neither Jew nor Greek, there is neither slave nor free, there is neither male nor female; for you are all one in Christ Jesus."

—Galatians 3:28

What do you think?

1. How could St. Paul suffer so much and yet be joyful?
2. In what ways do you keep in touch with your loved ones who live far away?
3. Can you say the Hail Mary? How does Mary help us?

BEHOLD, I STAND AT THE DOOR AND KNOCK;
IF ANYONE HEARS MY VOICE AND OPENS THE DOOR,
I WILL COME IN TO HIM AND EAT
WITH HIM, AND HE WITH ME.

—Revelation 3:20

Chapter Twenty-Four

The Kingdom of God Is Eternal

Revelation

The apostles spread the gospel all over the known world. They wrote letters to encourage the many churches. As the church grew, many more bishops, priests, and deacons were ordained. For many centuries up until the current day, the pope and the bishops have led the Church, teaching the Faith that springs from the Word of God. The Kingdom of God will continue even after the end of time. The final book of the Bible, Revelation, gives us a glimpse of eternity.

Bible Reading Checklist

- [ ] REVELATION 1; 3:14-22 John's first vision; letters to the churches
- [ ] REVELATION 4–5 The sacrificed Lamb is worshiped in heaven
- [ ] REVELATION 6–8:1 The coming judgment and the faithful people
- [ ] REVELATION 12:1-16; 19:1-16 The vision of Mary; the Wedding Supper
- [ ] REVELATION 20:1-10; 21–22 The Last Judgment

Introduction to Revelation

The book of Revelation helps us understand several parts of our faith, including the Mass, Mary, and the Last Judgment. The word *revelation* means "to show." It is written in an **apocalyptic** style. It uses symbols and images to connect current and future events with biblical events. Revelation is the last book of the Bible, and it may be the most difficult to understand. However, it is very important to try. It tells us how to truly worship God through the things John saw. It is as if John has pulled back a veil to reveal the covenant Bridegroom, Jesus, and his beautiful bride, the Church. Revelation provides encouragement to the Church when it faces difficult times.

John's First Vision

Revelation 1

The first Christians were persecuted for their belief in Jesus as the Son of God. Many people were suffering and dying in jails. In some places it was against the law to preach the gospel.

John was held prisoner on an island called Patmos. As John prayed on the Lord's Day, Sunday, he heard a voice and turned around to see one who was *"like a son of man"* (Daniel 7:13-14). The figure in the vision had eyes that glowed like fire, and he was holding seven stars. He was dressed in the clothing of a Jewish high priest. It was Jesus, walking among seven golden lampstands.

When John saw that it was Jesus, he fell at his feet in adoration. Jesus said, *"Fear not, I am the first and the last. I died but now I am alive forever"* (Revelation 1:17-18). He told John that the seven stars were the angels of seven churches, and the lampstands were those churches. Jesus told John to write seven letters, one to each church represented by the lampstands.

Letters to the Churches

Revelation 3:14-22

The letters to the seven churches encouraged them to remain faithful to God and told them to stop doing things that were wrong. They should remember that God will give eternal life in heaven to all who believe in Jesus Christ.

One of the letters was to the church in the city of Laodicea. Jesus said that the people in that church were "lukewarm." They were not cold or hot. Because of this, he was going to spit them out of his mouth. He meant that he wanted them to have a strong, enthusiastic love for God instead of halfhearted faith.

The people of Laodicea were rich and owned many nice things, but they were poor spiritually. That was because they thought they didn't need Jesus. In this letter are Jesus' comforting words: *"Behold, I stand at the door and knock; if anyone hears my voice and opens the door, I will come in to him and eat with him, and he with me"* (Revelation 3:20). We experience a foretaste of this heavenly banquet when we share the Eucharistic meal together at Mass.

The Sacrificial Lamb Is Worshiped in Heaven

Revelation 4–5

Jesus invited John to come up to heaven to experience what it is like. John entered through an open door. He saw a room in which God was seated on a throne. All heaven was worshiping God.

Around God's throne were the thrones of twenty-four elders, who represented the twelve tribes of Israel and the twelve apostles. Around God were four living creatures that looked like a lion, an ox, a man, and an eagle. Catholic Tradition says that these represent the four Gospel writers: Matthew, Mark, Luke, and John. The four creatures also show that believers in God will come from all four corners of the earth (see CCC 1137–1139). They were worshiping God, saying, ***"Holy, holy, holy is the Lord God Almighty"*** (Revelation 4:8).

John saw that the right hand of God held a scroll, rolled up and fastened with seven seals. Words were written on the scroll. The words were bad news for anyone who breaks the commandments.

An angel called out, "Who is worthy to open the scroll and break its seals?"

No one was found worthy until they saw the *"Lamb standing, as though it had been slain"* (Revelation 5:6). This was Jesus. Jesus is the Paschal (or Easter) Lamb. He was without sin but was sacrificed so we could be saved, just as an unblemished lamb was sacrificed on Passover (see Exodus 12).

The living creatures, the elders, and countless voices worshipped God, proclaiming, *"Worthy is the Lamb who was slain!"* (Revelation 5:12). Jesus is worthy to open the scroll because he obeyed God the Father completely. He became the perfect sacrificial Lamb, who died on the Cross to take away our sins.

The Coming Judgment and the Faithful People

Revelation 6–8:1

John saw Jesus open the seven sealed scrolls one at a time. Each time Jesus opened a seal, one of the four living creatures called, "Come forward." After the seal on the first scroll was broken, a white horse and rider approached. The rider was carrying a bow and wore a crown like a king. This rider represented Jesus, who would come as a powerful warrior and judge.

The next three scrolls brought horses and riders of a different kind. They symbolized the many bad things that would happen in the world because of sin, like sickness, fighting, and death.

The fifth scroll brought the martyrs: people who were killed because of their faith in Jesus. The sixth scroll brought a terrible earthquake, which represents the bad consequences of sin.

Before the seal on the seventh scroll was broken, an angel called out, "Do not harm anything until we put a seal on God's faithful ones!" Then a seal was placed on the foreheads of people who were faithful to God, to protect them from the trials to come. The sealed ones were those marked with the sign of faith. This is a sign that they belong to Christ as part of the communion of saints in heaven (see CCC 1296, 2159, 2642).

When the Lamb opened the seventh seal, there was silence. Suddenly the angels blew trumpets and threw fire down on the earth. There was lightning and thunder and an earthquake! Wars broke out, and there were plagues like those that had been inflicted on the Egyptians in the book of Exodus.

The Vision of Mary

Revelation 12:1-16

Another great sign was revealed to John—a woman in the sky! John describes her as one who was clothed with the sun. She had the moon under her feet and a crown of twelve stars on her head, and she was about to give birth. A huge red dragon wanted to devour her baby, because the woman's son was destined to rule the world. As soon as the child was born, he was taken up to God and his throne.

This woman is the Blessed Virgin Mary, who carried the child Jesus in her womb. Jesus is our Bread of Life, our High Priest, and the Word made flesh. The vision reminds us of the Ark of the Covenant in the Old Testament. The Ark carried manna (the saving food for the Israelites), Aaron's budding rod (symbolizing the high priest), and the stone tablets of the Ten Commandments (the Word of God). Mary carried Jesus, who is all of those things. As Queen of Heaven, Mary is a sign of hope and comfort to all of God's faithful people, who are his Church on earth.

THE ROSARY

Fifth Glorious Mystery

THE CORONATION OF MARY

(Revelation 12:1)

The Wedding Supper

Revelation 19:1-16

In John's vision, the angels in heaven sang praises to God as a great wedding took place. They were celebrating the marriage of the Lamb, who is Jesus, and his bride, the Church. The bride wore clothing of fine linen, bright and pure. This clothing signifies the righteous deeds of the saints.

God invites each of us to join him for a special banquet in the Marriage Supper of the Lamb. We get a foretaste of this feast when we celebrate the Eucharist. The Blessed Sacrament is food for our journey until we can celebrate the eternal banquet with God in heaven (see CCC 1244).

The angel told John to write this down: *"Blessed are those who are invited to the marriage supper of the Lamb"* (Revelation 19:9).

Each time we celebrate Mass, the saints and angels are there with us. The communion of saints includes all of us. It is the unity of all saints and believers on earth and in heaven who form one, holy, catholic, and apostolic Church (see CCC 960–962).

The Last Judgment

Revelation 20:1-10; 21–22

What John saw in the throne room in heaven was truly wonderful. He saw things that happen at the end of our earthly lives. He also saw the beginning of what is yet to come.

The Last Judgment is God's final victory over sin and death. As John continues to watch, he sees Satan thrown down into hell. Then all the saints and martyrs are raised from the dead and reign with Christ. Everyone whose name is found written in the book of life will joyfully live forever in heaven with Christ. Anyone whose name is not found in the book of life will be thrown into the lake of fire (see John 5:26-29).

Then John saw a beautiful vision of heaven. He saw a river flowing from the throne of God and the Lamb. The springs were full of life-giving water. This is God's grace. The Tree of Life was growing on the side of the river. Nothing sinful is there, only goodness. God and the Lamb, Jesus, are on the throne. The servants worship him there, and God's name is on their foreheads. There is no need for a lamp or sun because God is their light. God reigns forever.

The Bible ends with the word *amen*, which means "so be it" or "yes, it is so."

This is the Good News that God has wanted to share with us since the beginning of time—God is love! The story of salvation is our invitation to be friends with Jesus. We can have a relationship with him as part of the Church. The Church is his beloved bride. When you say yes to Jesus' invitation, you let him touch your heart. You let him feed you his Body, Blood, Soul, and Divinity in the Eucharist. Jesus wants to hold you in an intimate embrace.

The door to heaven has opened. You are invited. Will you eat at the table with the Lamb?

"He will come again in glory to judge the living and the dead
and his kingdom will have no end.
And I look forward to the resurrection of the dead
and the life of the world to come. Amen."

What do you think?

1. Have you ever imagined that there are angels and saints worshiping at Mass with you?
2. If Jesus knocked on your door, would you open the door and welcome him in? What would you say to him?
3. How do you create a holy heart for worshiping God?

Afterword

The Story Continues with You

Congratulations! You have read the story of salvation! This tells the story of the incredible love God has for you as shown through his Son, Jesus Christ, and in his Church. Jesus Christ is still working in the lives of people all around the world, just as he has since the beginning. We are now living in the period of "the Church." This is the final stage before Jesus comes again in glory to judge the living and the dead.

In the box below is the basic summary of the story of salvation. Now you can share it with others!

- God loves you and wants a relationship with you (see John 3:16).
- Sin has broken our relationship with God (see Genesis 3).
- Jesus Christ died to pay the penalty for your sins (see Romans 5:8).
- Believe in the gospel (see John 14:6-7; John 11:25-27).
- Repent, be baptized, and receive the Holy Spirit (see Acts 2:38).
- Live in Christ by keeping his commandments and remaining in communion with his body, the Church (see Matthew 5:3-9).
- Go and make disciples of Christ (see Matthew 28:19-20).

The following steps are necessary for being part of the **one**, **holy**, **catholic**, and **apostolic** Church:

1. **Receive the sacrament of Baptism:** To become a member of the Church, it is necessary to be baptized. Baptism is the sacrament that brings us from a life of sin to a life of holiness. (You were probably baptized as an infant.) After Baptism, the sacraments of Confirmation and Eucharist complete your initiation into the Church.

   Baptism ... now saves you, not as a removal of dirt from the body but as an appeal to God for a clear conscience, through the resurrection of Jesus Christ, who has gone into heaven and is at the right hand of God, with angels, authorities, and powers subject to him. – 1 Peter 3:21-22

2. **Celebrate the sacrament of Reconciliation:** We sometimes sin against God and others by doing what is wrong, so God has provided the sacrament of reconciliation—also called *confession*—to bring us back to the state of grace we received when we were baptized.

   If we confess our sins, he is faithful and just, and will forgive our sins and cleanse us from all unrighteousness. – 1 John 1:9

3. **Enter into the New Covenant through the Holy Eucharist:** Jesus has invited us into communion with him in the Eucharist, where he shares his very Body and Blood with those who are part of his Church. By receiving Jesus in the Holy Eucharist, we acknowledge Jesus as Lord and we draw strength to live a holy life.

   And he took bread, and when he had given thanks he broke it and gave it to them, saying, "This is my body which is given for you. Do this in remembrance of me." And likewise the cup after supper, saying, "This cup which is poured out for you is the new covenant in my blood." – Luke 22:19-20

4. **Pray**: To communicate with God, we need to speak and listen to him. A part of each day should be spent talking with God. There are books with prayers you can read, or you can simply have a conversation with God since he is your Father and a friend.

   Have no anxiety about anything, but in everything by prayer and supplication with thanksgiving let your requests be made known to God. – Philippians 4:6

5. **Live a life of charity:** To show others that you love Jesus, you need to live a life of charity, imitating the way Jesus and Mary lived on earth. They were truly loving and generous, and all that they did was to glorify God and to help other people. The life of charity includes living the virtues of faith, hope, and love, as well as prudence, temperance, fortitude, and justice (see CCC 1803–1829).

   A new commandment I give to you, that you love one another; even as I have loved you, that you also love one another. By this all men will know that you are my disciples, if you have love for one another. – John 13:34-35

6. **Teach others the story:** Continue to grow in your understanding of the Church's teachings through reading the Bible, the *Catechism of the Catholic Church*, and the writings of the popes and saints. With this knowledge and the power of the Holy Spirit, you can share with anyone how they can be part of the story, too!

   Go therefore and make disciples of all nations, baptizing them in the name of the Father and of the Son and of the Holy Spirit, teaching them to observe all that I have commanded you; and lo, I am with you always, to the close of the age." – Matthew 28:19-20

Glossary

AD – abbreviation of the Latin phrase *in anno Domini*, meaning "in the year of the Lord"; used with years following the birth of Jesus.

apocalyptic – a literary style in the Bible that uses symbolic terms and imagery to describe past, present, and future events. The book of Revelation and sections of Daniel are examples of apocalyptic literature in the Bible.

apostle – from a Greek word meaning "one who is sent"; the apostles were chosen by Jesus to go out and preach the gospel. This includes the original group of twelve chosen by Jesus, as well as Paul and Barnabas.

archaeologists – scientists who study the remains of buildings, artifacts, and bones from ancient times to learn about previous cultures.

Ark of the Covenant – also called the "Ark of God" or "Ark of the LORD"; built according to the instructions given by God to Moses; the gold-covered, wooden chest that held the Ten Commandments, Aaron's budding rod, and manna; carried by Levites on two poles during the time of the Tabernacle and later permanently placed in the "Holy of Holies" of the Temple in Jerusalem.

Asherah – a female fertility goddess worshiped by the Canaanites, usually represented in the form of a wooden pole.

Assumption, the – the bodily "taking up" of Mary into heaven at the end of her earthly life. In the words of Pope Pius XII when he defined this dogma in 1950, "Having completed the course of her earthly life, [Mary] was assumed body and soul into heavenly glory" (*Munificentissimus Deus*).

Assyria – a world power during the Divided Kingdom period of Bible history, located north of Israel in the region of Mesopotamia. The Assyrian army defeated the Northern Kingdom of Israel and took them into exile in 722 BC.

Assyrians – the people of Assyria.

Baal – a male Canaanite deity.

Babylon – a world power in Mesopotamia. The Babylonian army conquered Judah in 587 BC.

Babylonians – people of the Empire of Babylon.

Baptism – from a Greek word meaning "to immerse." Jesus commanded the apostles to "teach all nations, baptizing them in the name of the Father and of the Son and of the Holy Spirit" (Matthew 28:19). The baptism of John was a sign of repentance (see Matthew 3:11) that foreshadowed the sacrament of Baptism instituted by Christ.

BC – an abbreviation for "before Christ"; used with years before the birth of Jesus.

Book of the Law of Moses – the first five books of the Bible—Genesis, Exodus, Leviticus, Numbers, and Deuteronomy—which were once written on a single scroll; also called the Pentateuch ("five books"), the Torah, the Book of the Law, or the Law of Moses.

Canaan – the land promised to Abraham as an inheritance; also called the "Levant," the "Promised Land," "Israel," and, in more recent times, "Palestine."

census – an official recording of the people living in a particular geographical region.

centurion – a Roman army officer who commanded a hundred soldiers.

cherubim – a Hebrew word for "angels." After God cast Adam and Eve out of the Garden of Eden, he placed cherubim to guard it (Genesis 3:24).

Christ – from a Greek word meaning "anointed one" (see Matthew 16:16; CCC 453); translation of the Hebrew word Messiah.

Christians – followers of Jesus Christ, who have been baptized in his name.

Church – in the New Testament, the Greek word *ekklesia* ("to call out of") is used to refer to the universal assembly of believers in Jesus. The Church was established by Christ. Its members include all baptized Christians who profess the same faith under the authority of Jesus Christ and of St. Peter, and, successively, the bishops of Rome with the college of bishops who, as a group, are successors to the apostles.

circumcision – a sign of God's covenant with the Jewish people.

covenant – an agreement between God and one or more people. Usually involves the swearing of an oath. (See "Six Covenants Established in the Bible" on pages 207-209).

deacons – men of good reputation chosen by the apostles to help serve the Church, especially the poor and widowed. Today, deacons are ordained to assist bishops and priests in their ministry by performing baptisms, officiating at marriages, assisting at Mass (particularly by reading the Gospel and preaching), and bringing Communion to those who are ill, among other duties.

Dead Sea Scrolls – a collection of scrolls, written between the third century BC and the first century AD, discovered hidden in caves around the Dead Sea between 1946 and 1956; these scrolls contain portions of nearly every book of the Old Testament (except Esther).

disciples – followers of Jesus.

Egypt – a world power in the ancient world in northern Africa, whose rule extended at times all the way north to Babylon. The seat of power, ruled by a Pharaoh worshiped as though he were a god, was located along the Nile River Delta. Egypt was a world power from the Early World period of Bible history to the Divided Kingdom period of Bible history.

Emmanuel – a biblical name that means "God with us." In the Old Testament, the prophet Isaiah predicted the birth of Jesus with his words, "Behold, a young woman shall conceive and bear a son, and shall call his name Immanuel" (Isaiah 7). In the New Testament, an angel of the Lord appears to Joseph, telling him his son will fulfill this prophecy (see Matthew 1:23).

Ethiopia – a country southeast of Egypt, also referred to as "Cush" in the Bible.

Eucharist – one of the seven sacraments of the Church (see "The Seven Sacraments" on pages 210-213).

eunuch – a male who is unable to produce children, often employed to protect women of status; for example, the Ethiopian eunuch in Acts 8 who guarded the queen of Ethiopia.

Feast of Booths – also called "Sukkoth" or "Tabernacles," one of the three pilgrimage festivals required by Jewish law to be celebrated every year. In Jesus' time, this fall festival was celebrated in Jerusalem. Families built booths or tents and lived in them for the week to remind them that their forefathers wandered in the wilderness (see Leviticus 23:33-36).

Feast of Passover – also called "Pesach," one of the three pilgrimage festivals required by Jewish law to be celebrated every year. In Jesus' time, this spring festival was celebrated in Jerusalem, where each family or group of families sacrificed a lamb and ate it with a meal that recalls the first Passover (see Exodus 12:1-20), when God delivered them from Egypt. During this festival, Jesus instituted the Eucharist at the Last Supper during the Passover meal. Then he suffered, died, and rose from the dead within the eight days of the Feast of the Passover.

Feast of Pentecost – also called "Shavuot" or the "Feast of the Weeks," one of the three pilgrimage festivals required by Jewish law to be celebrated every year. In Jesus' time, this summer festival occurred fifty days after Passover and was celebrated in Jerusalem. This feast commemorates the giving of the Torah, the five books of Moses, to Moses on Mount Sinai. For the Catholic Church, Pentecost commemorates the birthday of the Church through the outpouring of the Holy Spirit on the apostles.

Feast of Unleavened Bread – this feast is combined with the Feast of Passover. During this weeklong festival, all leavened food was removed from a Jewish home to remind them how they left Egypt in haste (Exodus 12:18-20).

Gamaliel – a prominent rabbi from the time of Jesus, who was a member of the Jewish Council, or Sanhedrin, and was somewhat favorable toward the apostles.

Gentile – a non-Jewish person.

Hanukkah – also called the "Festival of Lights" or the "Feast of Dedication." It is an eight-day Jewish holiday started at the time of the Maccabean Revolt to commemorate the rededication of the Temple. Jesus attended this feast in Jerusalem (see John 10:22-31) and told the Jewish leadership that he and his Father are one. They tried to stone him for saying that.

Hasmoneans – the dynasty of the Maccabean family that ruled from the time of the Maccabees until they were conquered by Herod the Great during the Maccabean Revolt period of Bible history.

Hellenism – the adoption of ancient Greek culture, language, art, and worship.

I AM WHO I AM – the holy name of God, which was first spoken to Moses. "I AM WHO I AM" is the English translation of the four-letter Hebrew word YHWH (commonly pronounced as "Yahweh"). In traditional Judaism, this name is considered too holy to be spoken. Throughout the Old Testament, the Hebrew word Adonai ("LORD") is substituted for YHWH as a sign of reverence.

incarnate – the word describing the event of God the Father's Son, while remaining God, becoming fully a human being. Jesus Christ is true God and true man. In him there is a perfect union of divine nature and human nature in a divine Person (see CCC 464).

inspired – in the context of Scripture, it means "God breathed." Under the inspiration of the Holy Spirit, the human authors of the Bible—freely using their own intellect and abilities—wrote down "the truth which God, for the sake of our salvation, wished to see confided to the Sacred Scripture" (CCC 107); and so, their words are the words of God.

intercession – a type of prayer in which we place the needs of others before God. When someone says, "I'll pray for you," they are offering to be intercessors. When we bring our requests to Our Lady, the saints, and our guardian angels, they become our intercessors; they pray to God on behalf of those on earth in the same way that Jesus prays to the Father for us (see CCC 2635).

Ishmaelite – a descendant of Ishmael, son of Abraham and the slave woman Hagar, the older half brother of Isaac. Ishmael was sent away with his mother to live in Egypt after Isaac was born because Ishmael was not the child promised to Abraham and Sarah by God (see Genesis 16; 21:1-22).

Israelite – a descendant of the patriarch Jacob, also known as "Israel." Other common names used in the Bible for the Israelites are "Hebrews" or "children of Israel."

Jerusalem – the capital of Israel, located in Judah. Also called the "Holy City" because that is where King Solomon built the Temple. In the time of Abraham, the city was known as "Salem." In the time of David, it was occupied by the Jebusites, but David conquered it, and it became his capital.

Jew – a person who is a descendant of the tribe of Judah. After the Exile period of Bible history, those who returned to Jerusalem were called "Jews." Jesus was born of this lineage.

Judea – the geographic region where the tribe of Judah settled after the conquest of Canaan. It is the hilly region of Israel between the Mediterranean Sea and the Dead Sea. At the time of Jesus, this area was a province of Rome.

Lebanon – the nation to the north of Israel, or Canaan, known for its cedar forests.

lepers – people who contracted the disease of leprosy were considered "unclean" according to the Law of Moses and had to live outside of the camp or city in a group by themselves.

Maccabees – a family group of Jews that revolted against the Seleucid king Antiochus Epiphanes. The priest Mattathias first refused to break the Law of Moses. He had several sons that were also involved in what became known as the "Maccabean Revolt." Judas Maccabeus was the most prominent son and had the nickname of the "hammer."

Magi – an Old-Persian word designating the priest-astronomers who presided over the Persian religion. They were familiar with the Hebrew Scriptures.

manger – a feeding trough for animals. In biblical times, a manger was usually made from stone or wood.

manna – the heavenly food provided by God to sustain the Israelites during the Desert Wanderings period. It was white, sweet, and could be made into cakes. After the Israelites entered the Promised Land, manna was no longer provided; however, one jar of it was saved in the Ark of the Covenant.

martyr – someone who gives his or her life to defend his or her faith. They may be killed outright or caused to die by other circumstances related to defending their faith. "Martyr" comes from the Greek word meaning "witness." For Christians, a martyr is someone who is killed for defending his or her belief in Jesus.

Megiddo – an ancient city in northern Israel that overlooked and defended a trade route passing from Egypt to Mesopotamia. Many battles were fought at Megiddo between the various ancient powers. The valley below this city, Armageddon, is said to be the place of the last earthly battle (see Revelation 16:12-16). Megiddo is currently an archeological site.

Messiah – this word means "anointed one" in Hebrew; the one who would deliver the Jewish people from oppression. Jesus is understood in Christianity to be the Messiah predicted in the Old Testament. The word Christ is from the Greek word for Messiah.

monastery – usually a place of residence for monks or nuns who are living in seclusion under religious vow.

Moriah – a mountain range in the area of Judah that runs through Jerusalem, where Abraham offers Isaac. It is believed that the location of the sacrifice of Abraham is where the Temple Mount was built in Jerusalem. The name "Zion" is also used for this mountainous area of Jerusalem.

Mount Sinai – an important mountain in the Bible, located in the wilderness between Egypt and the Promised Land. The Israelites camped at this mountain after leaving Egypt, and Moses received the Ten Commandments there. It was also the location of the burning bush and where Elijah hears the "still small voice" of God (1 Kings 19:8-14). Sinai is also called Mount Horeb, "the mountain of God," where Moses brought water from the rock. The exact location of Mount Sinai is unknown, but the traditional site near St. Catherine's Monastery is a place of pilgrimage and is visited by thousands every year.

mythological – based on myths or fables.

Nazirite – a person who has taken a special vow to be set apart for God's service. A sign of the vow is that they do not cut their hair, they do not consume anything made from grapes, and they do not touch the deceased.

original sin – due to the sin of our first parents (Adam and Eve), we inherit the "stain" of original sin, meaning we are born in a "state of sin" and need redemption. Baptism purifies us from original sin; it brings us into the life of grace and makes us members of the Church. Mary was the only human person who was conceived and born without original sin, by a unique ("singular") grace of God, so that she would be prepared to be the mother of the God-man, Jesus (see CCC 490–493).

Passion, the – refers to the time of suffering from Jesus' agony in the Garden of Gethsemane through his arrest, trial, and crucifixion.

persecution – intentional harassment or abuse of a person or group of people by another person or group, often due to a conflict in religious belief or practice.

Persia – a world power during the Exile period of Bible history. Persia conquered Babylon and was later conquered by Greece in 334 BC. Much of the Persian Empire is now the modern country of Iran.

Pharisees – members of a Jewish religious group that strictly followed the laws of Moses. What they believed was good, but the way they lived their beliefs was not, according to Jesus (see Matthew 23:1-7).

plagues – a series of debilitating catastrophes that fell upon the Egyptians because of the refusal of Pharaoh to let the Israelites go and worship God. There were ten plagues in all, the last being the death of the firstborn.

Pope – the bishop of Rome. As the visible head of the Church, he is also called the "Vicar of Christ" and the "Roman Pontiff." He is traditionally referred to as the "Holy Father" or "His Holiness." The first pope was the apostle St. Peter, followed by 265 successors down to Pope Francis, the 266th pope.

prodigal – someone who is wasteful in spending; the term has come to mean "wayward" in describing the son who is welcomed back by his father in Jesus' parable of the Prodigal Son.

Promised Land – the territory that God promised to give Abraham. Other terms for the general geographical area are "Israel," "Canaan," the "Levant," and "Palestine."

prophets – persons chosen by God to proclaim the will of God and call people to live according to the covenant. Prophets sometimes tell what can happen in the future. In biblical times, they often played an important role as inspired advisors to kings. Besides prophets who spoke for God, there are also false prophets, such as the prophets involved in the worship of Baal.

Purim – a Jewish festival that commemorates Queen Esther for saving the Jewish people from extermination during the Exile period of Bible history.

repentance – sorrow for having done something wrong along with the desire to amend one's life and do right in the future.

Sabbath – the seventh day of Creation when God rested. God required people to rest from their labors on the seventh day. Since the resurrection of Jesus was on the first day of the week, the Church sets aside Sunday as a special day of rest. Sunday is also called the "Lord's Day," referring to the Resurrection.

sacrament – a sacred sign instituted by God to give grace. The seven sacraments were given to us by Jesus himself to celebrate and be drawn into a closer relationship with God himself. (See "The Seven Sacraments" on pages 210-213.)

Sadducees – members of a Jewish group at the time of Jesus that did not believe in the resurrection of the dead or the existence of spirits. They also did not believe in Jewish oral tradition, and they only accepted the written Law as binding on Jews. They were often at odds with the Pharisees.

Salvation History – looks to Sacred Scripture which is the inspired record of how God reveals himself to humanity in words and deeds. Starting in Genesis, God progressively shows who he is through events that are recognizable to humanity. This unique history culminates in Jesus Christ, who completely reveals the Father. Our response to God's revelation is the obedience of faith. Keeping with how God revealed himself in words and deeds, our response is also made up of words and deeds. With an understanding of salvation history, modern man moves forward with a better understanding of how to interact with God.

Samaritans – people who lived in the area of Samaria, in the area given to the tribe of Ephraim. At the time of Christ, the people who lived there were not considered Jews, but their religious worship was similar. The Samaritans were descendants of the Northern Kingdom of Israel mixed with people from five nations brought to occupy the area of Samaria during the Exile period of Bible history.

scribes – Jewish religious leaders who were experts in the Law and who helped hand on the traditions of Judaism.

Son of Man – a biblical expression that was used by the LORD when he spoke to the prophet Ezekiel. It also refers to an important person in Daniel's vision (see Daniel 7:12-13), one who would stand before God and have dominion over all things for all time. Jesus called himself the Son of Man, showing that he was the fulfillment of Daniel's prophecy.

swaddling clothes – strips of cloth used to wrap a baby.

synagogue – a building used for Jewish worship and study. Jesus read from the Bible in the synagogue in Nazareth and taught at many synagogues around the Sea of Galilee. On their journeys, the apostles would stop at synagogues to teach about Jesus.

Tabernacle – a portable tent used for worship that housed the Ark of the Covenant. This colorful tent was handcrafted by the Israelites during the time of the Desert Wanderings using the instructions that Moses received from God on Mount Sinai. The tribe of Levi was in charge of the Tabernacle and its furnishings, and the Levites transported the Tabernacle when the Israelite camp moved. This structure was used for worship until the first Temple was built in Jerusalem by King Solomon. Also referred to as the "Tent of Meeting," the "Dwelling," or the "Sanctuary."

Trinity – the Blessed Trinity is the central mystery of the Christian Faith (see CCC 243, 253), the belief that the Father, the Son, and the Holy Spirit are three distinct Persons who possess in common one single divine nature.

unclean spirits – angels that have fallen and do the work of the devil; also called "evil spirits" or "demons."

Vatican II – also known as the "Second Vatican Council." One of the twenty-one ecumenical councils held in the history of the Church, Vatican II met from 1962 to 1965. An ecumenical council is a gathering of the bishops of the Church, called together (or at least approved) by the pope. An important document issued by Vatican II is Dei Verbum ("The Word of God"), which discusses divine revelation as it is contained in the Bible and Sacred Tradition and how this revelation is handed on to every generation.

veil of the Temple – a thick woven curtain that separated the Holy of Holies—the innermost room of the Temple that contained the Ark of the Covenant—from the "Holy Place," the outer room. This veil was made of heavy red and purple yarn and embroidered with cherubim angels. During Christ's crucifixion, the veil being torn in two signified that Jewish Temple worship was being replaced by the new Temple, the body of Christ, the Church, which would include all peoples.

womb – a place in a woman's body where babies grow before birth; the "uterus."

Yahweh - The term used to refer to the divine name of God that was revealed to Moses. In the Hebrew language it means "I Am Who I Am."

Zion – a term used to mean the mountain of the LORD or the place where God is present. The holy city of Jerusalem is also called "Zion."

Appendix

The Six Covenants

A covenant in the Bible is an agreement between God and an individual or group. Everyone who is part of the covenant makes a solemn promise to agree to its terms and swears an oath to be faithful to it. Both parties agree to keep their promise, even if this means suffering or dying. God's relationship with us has developed through a progression of six covenants described in the Bible. The progression began with two people—Adam and Eve—and has grown to include all people who are members of the Church.

The First Covenant **One Holy Couple**

Covenant with Adam and Eve (see Genesis 1–3)

God established his first covenant with Adam and Eve, the first man and woman who were united in marriage, *One Holy Couple*. From their union, the world would be blessed. The Sabbath day of rest was given to Adam and Eve as a sign to rest from their labor and to commune with God. The covenant of marriage and the sign of the Sabbath are linked with Creation. It is fitting that marriage is linked with Creation, as it is here that new life begins. Marriage is the foundation of a family unit.

The Second Covenant **One Holy Family**

Covenant with Noah and his family (see Genesis 9)

After the great Flood, Noah and his family came out of the ark and saw a rainbow in the sky. This rainbow was given by God as the sign of the second covenant he made with his people. God promised Noah that he would never again destroy the whole earth with a flood. This covenant with Noah and his family is *One Holy Family*. They would learn how to love and obey God as they again filled the earth with children and grandchildren.

The Third Covenant **One Holy Tribe**

Covenant with Abraham (see Genesis 15, 17, 22)

God made a covenant with Abram, promising him that he would have as many descendants as there are stars in the sky. Abram was ninety-nine years old, yet miraculously, this promise came true with the birth of Isaac. The third covenant that God made with his people is *One Holy Tribe.* God also promised to give Abram land and a royal dynasty. As a sign of this covenant, God changed Abram's name to Abraham. Abraham promised to dedicate to God through circumcision all his male children and grandchildren and all the following generations and to obey all of God's laws. Circumcision is the sign of the covenant.

The Fourth Covenant **One Holy Nation**

Covenant with Moses (see Exodus 24, Deuteronomy 29)

After God delivered the Israelites from the bondage of Egypt through the Passover, the Israelites stood at the foot of Mount Sinai, where Moses sacrificed young bulls and sprinkled some of the blood on the people, saying, "This is the blood of the covenant which the LORD has made with you." God promised to make them a mighty nation of priests, *One Holy Nation.* The people agreed to obey all that the LORD had commanded them to do. As a sign of this covenant, God gave Moses two tablets of stone with the Ten Commandments written on them. All the Israelites except for the tribe of Levi broke this covenant by worshiping an idol; consequently, only Levites served as priests. God still blessed the Israelites as a nation.

The Fifth Covenant **One Holy Kingdom**

Covenant with David (see 2 Samuel 7:11-15)

God made a covenant with King David, promising that he would give him a son who would build a house for the LORD and establish a kingdom for all the people. God promised that David's kingdom, *One Holy Kingdom,* would last forever and that he would not take his steadfast love away from him. The sign of this covenant is the Temple in Jerusalem, which was built by David's son Solomon. Jesus is the promised Messiah who came from David's royal line.

The Sixth Covenant **One Holy Church**

New Covenant with Christ (see Matthew 16:18; Luke 22:1-23)

Jesus' death on the cross, his resurrection, and his ascension into heaven fulfill God's promise of redemption made to Adam and Eve after their sin in the Garden of Eden. Jesus fulfills the conditions of the old covenant made on Mount Sinai and establishes the New Covenant. He was the perfect sacrifice who could at last break the power of sin and death over people. The Holy Eucharist is the eternal memorial of the New Covenant.

The New Covenant family of God is the body of Christ, the Church, *One Holy Church,* who by the power of the Holy Spirit can live the will of Christ here on earth. While all people who are baptized into Christ have a share in the Church, full communion involves sharing the bonds of faith, sacraments, and pastoral governance found in the teachings of the Catholic Church.

The Nicene Creed

The Nicene Creed is a confession of faith that was issued by the First Council of Nicaea in AD 325. It is recited at every Sunday Mass and on solemn feasts. Excerpts from the Nicene Creed have been placed into this Storybook at certain points to help children better understand what they recite each week at Mass.

> *I believe in one God, the Father almighty, maker of heaven and earth, of all things visible and invisible.* (Chapter Two)
>
> *I believe in one Lord Jesus Christ, the Only Begotten Son of God, born of the Father before all ages. God from God, Light from Light, true God from true God, begotten, not made, consubstantial with the Father; through him all things were made.* (Chapter Two)
>
> *For us men and for our salvation he came down from heaven* (bow), *and by the Holy Spirit was incarnate of the Virgin Mary, and became man.* (Chapter Eighteen)
>
> *For our sake he was crucified under Pontius Pilate, he suffered death and was buried, and rose again on the third day in accordance with the Scriptures.*

He ascended into heaven and is seated at the right hand of the Father. (Chapter Twenty)

He will come again in glory to judge the living and the dead and his kingdom will have no end. (Chapter Twenty-Four)

I believe in the Holy Spirit, the Lord, the giver of life, who proceeds from the Father and the Son, who with the Father and the Son is adored and glorified, who has spoken through the prophets. (Chapter Twenty-One)

I believe in one, holy, catholic, and apostolic Church. (Chapter Twenty-Two)

I confess one baptism for the forgiveness of sins and I look forward to the resurrection of the dead and the life of the world to come. Amen. (Chapter Twenty-Four)

The Seven Sacraments

The seven sacraments have been given to us by Jesus so that we can experience God's presence and his saving grace. Each sacrament is an outward sign of a greater inward reality that gives us God's grace to become closer to him and to do his work on earth.

Sacraments of Initiation

The three sacraments that provide the foundation for Christian life.

1. BAPTISM

Baptism is birth into new life in Christ (CCC 1277), the first sacrament of initiation—that is, the first step on our journey in the Faith. Baptism forgives sins and makes us members of the Church.

Signs and words: Water is poured on our heads (or we are immersed in it), as the words "I baptize you in the name of the Father, and of the Son, and of the Holy Spirit" are spoken by the priest or deacon.

Sacramental grace: Original sin and—if the person being baptized is beyond the age of reason—personal sins are forgiven, and we become a member of the Church.

Frequency: Once. It must be received before any other sacrament.

Bible verses: Matthew 28:19-20; John 3:3, 22; 4:1-2; Acts 2:38.

2. CONFIRMATION

In Confirmation, we receive an outpouring of the Holy Spirit in order to be a stronger member of the Church and a witness of faith (CCC 1316). This is one of the three sacraments of initiation.

Signs and words: A bishop anoints our foreheads with sacred oil (chrism) and says the words, "Be sealed with the Gift of the Holy Spirit" (CCC 1320).

Sacramental grace: We are strengthened by the Holy Spirit and become full members of the Church.

Frequency: Once. (In the United States, confirmation is usually received in middle school, but it may be received in high school in some dioceses. Adults converting to the Faith also receive confirmation as part of the Rite of Christian Initiation of Adults process.)

Bible verses: John 20:22; Acts 2:4, 8:14-17, 19:6; 2 Corinthians 1:21-22 (CCC 1296), 2 Corinthians 2:15 (CCC 1294).

3. THE HOLY EUCHARIST

The Eucharist is the real Body, Blood, Soul, and Divinity of Christ in the form of bread and wine (see CCC 1374). It is one of the three sacraments of initiation, the one in which we receive Christ himself and are united with all Catholics on earth and in heaven (see CCC 1326). Jesus gave us the Eucharist at the Last Supper with the same words used by the priest during the Liturgy of the Eucharist at Mass.

Signs and words: We eat and drink what appears to be bread and wine, which have changed into the Body and Blood of Christ through the consecration at Mass. The priest, deacon, or extraordinary minister holds up the host (or cup) and says, "The Body (or Blood) of Christ," and we reply, "Amen."

Sacramental grace: We are spiritually nourished by Christ's Body and Blood, and we are united "in communion" with Christ and all members of the Church.

Frequency: If we are in the state of grace, we are encouraged to receive Communion whenever we attend Mass (see CCC 1388). At minimum, a Catholic should receive the Eucharist at least once a year—if possible, during the Easter season (see CCC 1389).

Bible verses: Matthew 26:26-29; Mark 14:22-25; Luke 22:14-20; John 6:48-58; Acts 20:7.

Sacraments of Healing

4. RECONCILIATION (also called Penance or Confession)

In the sacrament of Reconciliation, we receive God's forgiveness for our sins. We confess our sins and express sorrow over them. We perform an act of penance and acknowledge the desire to avoid sin in the future. Broken relationships are healed through confession.

Signs and words: We confess our sins to a priest, and we resolve to perform the penance for them given to us by him. The priest, acting with the authority given to him by Christ himself through his ordination, administers God's forgiveness with the words of absolution: "I absolve you from your sins in the name of the Father, and of the Son, and of the Holy Spirit."

Sacramental grace: Our sins are forgiven, and we are reconciled with God and the Church.

Frequency: Reconciliation may be received as often as we need it throughout our lives, but we are required to confess any mortal sins before receiving Communion. Some people go to confession every week as an act of devotion to receive God's grace and be strengthened in virtue, even though they may have only venial sins to confess. The Church teaches we must go to confession at least once a year during Lent, in preparation for Easter.

Bible verses: Matthew 16:19, 18:18; John 20:22-23; James 5:16.

5. ANOINTING OF THE SICK

A priest anoints the forehead and hands of the sick person with blessed oil, praying for his or her physical and spiritual healing.

Signs and words: Blessed oil is used to anoint the forehead and hands of a sick person with the prayer, "Through this holy anointing may the Lord in his love and mercy help you with the grace of the Holy Spirit. May the Lord who frees you from sin save you and raise you up."

Sacramental grace: The sick person is strengthened in his or her time of illness and prepared to enter eternal life.

Frequency: Anointing of the sick may be received whenever we are seriously ill.

Bible verses: Mark 6:7-13; Luke 9:2; James 5:14-16.

Sacraments of Service

6. HOLY ORDERS

To continue the ministry Jesus gave to the first apostles, the sacrament of Holy Orders is given to men who are called to serve his people as deacons, priests, or bishops.

Signs and words: A bishop lays his hands upon the head of the man being ordained and says a special prayer of consecration, asking God to send the Holy Spirit to help the new priest or deacon to perform the duties of his office (CCC 1573).

Sacramental grace: Through ordination, deacons, priests, and bishops are given a special sacramental "seal" (or mark) that gives them the power to act with the authority of Jesus himself.

Frequency: A man can only be ordained once to each of the three levels (or "degrees") of holy orders—deacon, priest, and bishop. This sacrament may only be received by a baptized man (CCC 1598).

Bible verses: Mark 3:13-19; Luke 5:10-11; John 20:21-23; Acts 6:6; 1 Timothy 4:14, 5:22; 2 Timothy 1:6.

7. MATRIMONY (or Marriage)

The sacrament of Matrimony, or marriage, is a public sign of the loving union of a man and a woman for life, celebrated in a Mass. The man and woman give themselves to each other and remain open to having children (CCC 1601).

Signs and words: In the Roman rite of the Church, a husband and wife marry each other when they profess their vows in the presence of a priest or deacon and two other witnesses.

Sacramental grace: The couple is united to each other, and they become "one flesh." They receive God's grace to love each other and to welcome and educate their children. The sacrament of marriage may only be received by two baptized Christians.

Frequency: Once, unless one of the spouses dies or the marriage is declared invalid by the Church. When a spouse dies, the other spouse is free to marry.

Bible verses: Genesis 1:27-28, 2:18-25; Matthew 19:4-6; Ephesians 5:20-33.

Scriptural Origins of the Rosary

The Rosary is a traditional and popular devotion that consists of a set of beautiful prayers recited aloud while holding a rosary: a set of beads used to keep track of each prayer. The Rosary begins with the Sign of the Cross and the Apostles' Creed, followed by the prayers of the Our Father, the Hail Mary, and the Glory Be. (Other prayers are sometimes added.) While praying each decade of Hail Marys, one should meditate upon each mystery. The mysteries are biblical events from the lives of Jesus and Mary.

Sign of the Cross (Matthew 28:19)

In the name of the Father, and of the Son, and of the Holy Spirit. Amen.

Our Father (Matthew 6:9-13)

Our Father, who art in heaven, hallowed be thy name; thy kingdom come, thy will be done, on earth as it is in heaven. Give us this day our daily bread, and forgive us our trespasses as we forgive those who trespass against us; and lead us not into temptation, but deliver us from evil. Amen.

Hail Mary

Hail Mary, full of grace, the Lord is with you. (Luke 1:28)
Blessed are you among women, and blessed is the fruit of your womb, Jesus. (Luke 1:42)
Holy Mary, Mother of God, pray for us sinners, now and at the hour of our death. Amen.

Mysteries of the Rosary

Joyful Mysteries (Storybook Chapter Eighteen)

The Annunciation (Luke 1:28)

The Visitation (Luke 1:41-42)

The Birth of Christ (Luke 2:7)

The Presentation of Jesus (Luke 2:22-23)

The Finding of the Child Jesus in the Temple (Luke 2:48)

Luminous Mysteries (Storybook Chapters Eighteen and Twenty)

The Baptism of Jesus (Luke 3:22)

The Wedding at Cana (John 2:1-11)

The Proclamation of the Kingdom (Matthew 5:1-12)

The Transfiguration (Luke 9:28-36)

The Institution of the Eucharist (Luke 22:19-20)

Sorrowful Mysteries (Storybook Chapter Twenty)

The Agony in the Garden (Luke 22:44-45)

The Scourging at the Pillar (John 19:1)

The Crowning with Thorns (Matthew 27:28-29)

Jesus Carries the Cross (John 19:17)

The Crucifixion (Luke 23:46)

Glorious Mysteries (Storybook Chapters Twenty, Twenty-One, Twenty-Three, and Twenty-Four)

The Resurrection of Christ (Luke 24:1-7)

The Ascension (Luke 24:51)

The Descent of the Holy Spirit (Acts 2:4)

The Assumption of Mary into Heaven (CCC 966)

The Coronation of Mary (Revelation 12:1)

Scripture Quotes Used in Mass

Penitential Act

Mass Phrase: *"Lord have mercy. Christ have mercy. Lord have mercy."* (Found in Chapter Nineteen)

Scripture Quote: *"Lord have mercy on us, Son of David"* (Matthew 20:31).

Gloria

Mass Phrase: *"Glory to God in the highest, and on earth peace to people of good will."* (Found in Chapter Eighteen)

Scripture Quote: *"Glory to God in the highest, and on earth peace among men with whom he is pleased"* (Luke 2:14).

Liturgy of the Word

First Reading: from the Old Testament (or from the book of Acts during the Easter Season)

Responsorial Psalm: from the book of Psalms

Second Reading: from the New Testament other than the Gospels

The Gospel: from Matthew, Mark, Luke, or John

Eucharistic Prayer

Sanctus:

Mass Phrase: *"Holy, Holy, Holy Lord God of hosts. Heaven and earth are full of your glory. Hosanna in the highest. Blessed is he who comes in the name of the Lord. Hosanna in the highest."* (Found in Chapter Twenty)

Scripture Quote: *"Holy, holy, holy is the LORD of hosts; the whole earth is full of his glory"* (Isaiah 6:3). *"Blessed is he who comes in the name of the Lord! Hosanna in the highest!"* (Matthew 21:9; Luke 19:38).

Institution Narrative:

Mass Phrase: *"Take this, all of you, and eat of it: for this is my body which will be given up for you ... do this in memory of me."* (Found in Chapter Twenty)

Scripture Quote: *"This is my body which is given for you. Do this in remembrance of me"* (Luke 22:19).

Memorial Acclamation:

Mass Phrase: *"When we eat this Bread and drink this Cup, we proclaim your Death, O Lord, until you come again."*

Others Mentioned in the Bible

Scripture Quote: *"For as often as you eat this bread and drink the cup, you proclaim the Lord's death until he comes"* (1 Corinthians 11:26).

Great Amen:

Mass Phrase: *"Amen."* At the end of the Eucharistic prayer, we respond with the Great Amen.

Scripture Quote: "*Amen.*" Amen is used many times in the Bible and is the very last word at the end of the book of Revelation.

The Communion Rite

Lord's Prayer:

Mass Phrase and Scripture Quote: *The Our Father* (Matthew 6:9-13; found in Chapter Nineteen).

Sign of Peace:

Mass Phrase and Scripture Quote: *"Peace be with you"* (John 20:19, 21, found in Chapter Twenty).

Agnus Dei:

Mass Phrase: *"Lamb of God, you take away the sins of the world: have mercy on us.*
Lamb of God, you take away the sins of the world: have mercy on us.
Lamb of God, you take away the sins of the world: grant us peace."

Scripture Quote: *"The Lamb of God who takes away the sin of the world"* (John 1:29).

Reception of Communion:

Mass Phrase: *"Lord, I am not worthy that you should enter under my roof; but only say the word, and my soul shall be healed."* (Found in Chapter Eighteen)

Scripture Quote: *"Lord, I am not worthy to have you come under my roof; but only say the word, and my servant will be healed"* (Matthew 8:8).

Directory of the Apostles and Their Ministries

Name	Alternative Names/Titles	Place of Death (according to Tradition)	Author of:
Simon Peter	Cephas (Peter, "Rock"), son of John, son of Jonah	Martyred at Rome Buried beneath St. Peter's Basilica	1, 2 Peter
Andrew	Brother of Peter	Martyred at Patras	
James	Son of Zebedee, son of thunder, Boanerges, James the Greater, bishop of Jerusalem	Martyred at Jerusalem	James
John	Son of Zebedee, son of thunder, Boanerges, brother of James, the Beloved Disciple, the Evangelist	Exiled on the island of Patmos Died in Ephesus	Gospel of John; 1, 2, 3 John; Revelation
Philip	from Bethsaida	Martyred at Hierapolis	
Bartholomew	Nathaniel, son of Tomay, of Cana in Galilee	Martyred in Armenia	
Thomas	Doubting Thomas, Didymus, the Twin	Martyred in India	
Matthew	The tax collector, Levi, the son of Alphaeus, the Evangelist	Martyred at Ethiopia	Gospel of Matthew
James (the son of Alphaeus)	James the Less	Martyred at Ostrakine	
Simon (called the Zealot)	Simon the Cananaean	Martyred at Persia	
Judas (the son of James)	Thaddeus, Judas not Iscariot	Martyred at Persia	
Judas Iscariot (who betrayed Jesus)	Son of Perdition	Jerusalem; buried in Potter's Field	

Name	Alternative Names/Titles	Place of Death (according to Tradition)	Author of:
Matthias	Replacement for Judas Iscariot		
Paul	Saul	Martyred at Rome	Romans; 1, 2 Corinthians; Galatians; Ephesians; Philippians; Colossians; 1, 2 Thessalonians; 1, 2 Timothy; Titus; Philemon; Hebrews
Luke	The Evangelist, the Physician	Greece	Gospel of Luke; Acts
Mark	John Mark, the Evangelist	Martyred at Alexandria	Gospel of Mark

About the Authors

Emily Cavins

Emily has assisted her husband, Jeff, in the development of *The Bible Timeline: The Story of Salvation*. She is the author of *My Heart Is a Violin* and *Lily of the Mohawks: The Story of St. Kateri*. She is a contributing editor to *Amazing Grace for Mothers*. She received her degree in classical and Near Eastern archaeology from the University of Minnesota. Jeff and Emily have three daughters.

Lisa Bromschwig

Lisa is a convert to Catholicism and has a passion for Jesus in the Word and sacraments. She holds a master's degree in pastoral ministry from St. Paul Seminary in St. Paul, Minnesota, and has worked as a director of religious education in Catholic parishes. She has served as a catechist in Catholic religious education programs and a substitute teacher in Catholic schools. Lisa and her husband, Kurt, have three children.

Regina Lickteig Neville

Regina received her bachelor's degree in education and theater liberal arts from the University of Northern Iowa and a master of fine arts degree from Yale University. She has managed many nonprofit arts and education organizations in addition to working directly with students. Regina has served as a director of religious education and taught faith formation for more than fifteen years. Regina and her husband, Tom, have three children.

Linda Wandrei

Linda is a full-time wife and mother. She received her bachelor's degree in business administration from the University of St. Thomas, St. Paul, Minnesota. She has catechized children from preschool to sixth grade in local parishes and vacation Bible school programs for the past twenty years. She also served as a Bible study coordinator for Jeff Cavins' *Great Adventure* series "Adventures in the Acts of the Apostles." Linda was raised Catholic and was inspired to teach her children the fullness of truth and love on which the Catholic Church is built. She and her husband, Phil, have three children.